THE ECONOMICS OF BENCHMARKING

Other books by the same author:

Input–Output Economics: Theory and Applications – Featuring Asian Economies, World Scientific Publishing, 2009

The Economics of Input–Output Analysis, Cambridge University Press, 2006

Structural Economics, Routledge, 2004

The Growth of Service Industries – The Paradox of Exploding Costs and Persistent Demand, edited with R. Schettkat, Edward Elgar, 2001

Linear Analysis of Competitive Economies, Prentice Hall/Harvester Wheatsheaf, 1995

THE ECONOMICS OF BENCHMARKING

MEASURING PERFORMANCE FOR COMPETITIVE ADVANTAGE

THIJS TEN RAA
TILBURG UNIVERSITY, THE NETHERLANDS

First published 2009 by
PALGRAVE MACMILLAN

Palgrave Macmillan in the UK is an imprint of Macmillan Publishers Limited, registered in England, company number 785998, of Houndmills, Basingstoke, Hampshire RG21 6XS.

Palgrave Macmillan in the US is a division of St Martin's Press LLC, 175 Fifth Avenue, New York, NY 10010.

Palgrave Macmillan is the global academic imprint of the above companies and has companies and representatives throughout the world.

Palgrave® and Macmillan® are registered trademarks in the United States, the United Kingdom, Europe and other countries.

ISBN-13: 978-0-230-22438-4
ISBN-10: 0-230-22438-5

This book is printed on paper suitable for recycling and made from fully managed and sustained forest sources. Logging, pulping and manufacturing processes are expected to conform to the environmental regulations of the country of origin.

A catalogue record for this book is available from the British Library.

A catalog record for this book is available from the Library of Congress.

10 9 8 7 6 5 4 3 2 1
18 17 16 15 14 13 12 11 10 09

Printed and bound in China

CONTENTS

FIGURES

TABLES

There are three kinds of lies: lies, damned lies, and statistics.

Benjamin Disraeli

There are lies, damn lies, and benchmarks.

after Mark Twain

I dedicate this book to William J. Baumol, my benchmark.

PREFACE

Benjamin Disraeli's observation that "There are three kinds of lies: lies, damned lies, and statistics" was right and still is, nearly two centuries after he was prime minister of Britain. The fad of benchmarking has spread from politics to business and back to politics; Senator Ted Kennedy quipped on U.S. involvement in Iraq that "We ought to have a benchmark where the administration has to come back and give us a report." Following Mark Twain's paraphrase, I would say that *benchmarking is the elevated art of lying with statistics*. Benchmarking is not only a quantitative decision tool to support rational decision making, but even has the capacity to obscure the underlying concepts. What is a benchmark? In business terms, are we talking productivity, efficiency, profitability, or what?

Benchmarking involves the comparison between business units or firms. The comparison is usually in terms of the costs of processes and operations, but may also involve output performance measures, such as volume and quality measures. The tool of benchmarking is applied widely. The exceptions, businesses that do not engage in benchmarking, tend to be the very small ones. Many small businesses simply do not have the resources for such a management tool, and if they need it, they may outsource it. Like accounting activities, benchmarking can be purchased off the shelves, from consultancies, or even in the form of ready-to-use software.

Benchmarking is simple if there is a single agreed-upon criterion. This is rare, but let us assume for a moment that there is one, say profitability. In this case we evaluate all business units we want to compare by profitability and rank them accordingly. This simple rating procedure yields a #1, called the *best practice* or *benchmark*, and a #last, the black sheep. The idea and frequent use of benchmarking is not only to identify the best practice, but also to copy it. When the Japanese replaced the Americans as leading automobile makers, their high-quality cars were taken apart and reassembled just to understand how they did it. On top of this Japanese plants were frequently visited by Europeans and Americans to learn their production processes. This was benchmarking *avant la lettre*.

If there are multiple criteria—for example also shareholder's value or even more long-run variables such as customer satisfaction—benchmarking can still be done, but the results might not be clear. Different units may score best in different dimensions. The more narrowly defined benchmarking is an operations research tool that pushes through the idea of naming and shaming in settings where there are different, possibly conflicting scores. This is the domain of consultants, who use fancy mathematical techniques, but this book opens the playground to the general public, or at least to people who read business books. I shall do so by developing an economic approach to the subject matter, a procedure that provides weights or prices to the alternative scores. This way we can aggregate different scores and get back into the simple, straightforward comparison world of benchmarking.

To explain the theme and organization of the book let me pose a seemingly vague but important question: what to do with a business unit that scores well in one dimension but is poor in another? Stimulate the business unit to excel in both aspects, by helping it to do better where it is weak? Or let it specialize in what it is good at and cut the weak spot? Often there are trade-offs, and it may just be too costly to score best in all respects. This logic may even become inescapable. For example, if the value–price ratio constitutes a performance dimension, it is bound to go down as other performance aspects are enhanced. Improvements of other scores (human resources, name recognition, or whatever) are bound to be costly, increase the price, and thus depress the value–price ratio by the denominator effect. Another example of a score trade-off is between cost and quality. Excessive emphasis on cost reductions goes at the expense of quality performance, and conversely, quality improvements have price tags. There are trade-offs between alternative scores. Compromises have to be found, and different score dimensions must be weighed by the management.

The situation is reminiscent of the classical economic problem of the allocation and pricing of scarce resources for alternative ends. Economic theory shows how the interplay between demand and supply creates scarcities, and how equilibrium is attained by pricing resources according to their scarcity, and goods and services by the value of their resource contents. These contents are determined by the state of technology. By a slight twist of the mind we shall be able to apply the formal structure of this economic approach to the problem of weighting alternative business objectives.

In principle weights can be preset to formulate an overall performance measure, but subtle issues emerge. For example, if you want to rank businesses, you had better use a uniform set of weights for performance components across the businesses you compare. This book explains how potentially conflicting performance aspects can be balanced by assigning rational weights to aspects. The analysis is applicable at the industry level—when analysts want to rank competing firms—and also at the company level—where management wants to improve the performance of business units.

Another distinction is between internal and external or competitive benchmarking. *Internal benchmarking* helps to spot exemplary business units within big companies, such as hotel chains. It identifies the relevant benchmarks for every unit, suggests cost components that can be cut and potential revenue sources that would boost performance. *External benchmarking* includes competition in the pool of examples, and is therefore also called *competitive* benchmarking. It is a more demanding management tool, if only because data are hard to get from competitors, but potentially more rewarding. If you extend the pool with which you compare, the benchmark will be better, and therefore the achievement level higher.

The extension of benchmarking beyond a simple, one-dimensional rating exercise makes it a powerful management tool.

Among other things, it solves the puzzle of making sense out of different scores in different dimensions, such as the volume of sales and the level of quality. It facilitates multi-dimensional comparisons. Perhaps the most important application is a little-known one. The performance of an organization is more than the sum of the parts. Benchmarking can be used not only to improve underperforming business units, but also to reallocate resources in the company.

There is an interesting connection between the fine-tuning of an organization by reallocations and rewards. Roughly speaking, we shall show that resources are better reallocated to the more efficient business units. While this makes sense from the viewpoint of production process performance optimization, it also provides the right incentives. Most managers appreciate it when their control over company resources is extended. If benchmarking is an integrated management tool, this yields an incentive to run business units efficiently, on top of financial bonus plans. The two can be combined. Benchmarking is used not only to weed out production and organization inefficiencies, but also to design bonus plans.

Benchmarking is a particularly useful tool for organizations where market prices are missing, either on the output side (e.g. for contributions to quality of life aspects) or the input side (such as for volunteers' work). This includes nonprofit organizations.[1] Market prices constitute natural weights for performance measurement and are the foundation of accounting indeed, but a good substitute can be developed and that is one of the objectives of this book.

The technique I use is *data envelopment analysis* (DEA). DEA is a simple benchmarking tool, but unfortunately little applied by managers. One doubt about it has been articulated by Schefczyk (1993), a reliable source, who has used the tool extensively to analyze the performance of airlines. He wrote that a disadvantage of DEA is that:

---

1 See Speckbacher (2003, pp. 269–70).

in a multiproduct case, the production function can neither associate specific inputs with specific outputs, nor can it determine the relative importance of individual outputs for performance.

While this statement did characterize the state of the art in the 1990s, the determination of the relative importance of alternative outputs or scores is now within reach. This is true even within the narrowly defined benchmarking framework of DEA, and I shall detail how weights can be assigned.

Benchmarking, particularly DEA-based benchmarking, is yet to be integrated with other management tools. The airline industry is perhaps the one with the most widespread use of benchmarking. Here managers routinely measure the performance of their company in comparison with the competition, and consumers visit websites to compare not only prices but also flight statistics, to assess costs and value aspects, such as the reliability of departure and arrival times. Nonetheless, Francis, Humphreys and Fry (2005) report that benchmarking is the most popular performance measurement tool in the industry, but that only one airline beefs it up with DEA. The perceived incapacity to value alternative performance components may be a hurdle, and we shall overcome it.

Most applications of benchmarking are basically alternative performance measurements and rankings, both financial and non-financial, and the bulk are based on output scores, such as revenues, net earnings, and customer satisfaction. I find it important though to bring in the inputs, if only to separate size effects from true performance scores. I do so throughout the book, and we shall encounter a number of interesting findings. For example, the use of output to input value ratios will emerge as a natural performance measure, instead of difference-based level concepts, such as profit (which is revenue minus cost). There is a close connection between the subtle distinction between ratios and difference on one hand, and the distinction between the concepts of efficiency, productivity, and profitability on the other. All this tends to be a smorgasbord in the business literature, and it is high time to disentangle the concepts and to clarify which is appropriate for performance measurement and ranking. This book provides the analysis. Moreover, it will be able to bring in non-financial output and input measures. Perhaps surprisingly, even such alternative measures can be subjected to quantitative scrutiny. The measurement of their importance is an integral part of benchmarking analysis as developed in this book.

While the intended readership are undergraduate BA/beginning MBA students, the book should appeal to non-academic readers as well. To accommodate a wide audience, I have made it self-contained. I have not assumed any prior knowledge. Some experience with Microsoft's Excel® program would be handy, but even that is not necessary. If you persist in reading the book closely—reading slowly when some formulas are introduced or graphs are discussed—the rewards will be great. You will have mastered the basic ideas which hitherto have been confined to technical operations research texts, without having to wade through a morass of mathematics and statistics. Yet you will master just enough to be able to understand and apply the techniques.

Let me give a roadmap of the book. **Chapter 1** outlines the different types of benchmarking, ranging from simple score comparisons to operations research tools. It also distinguishes levels of management and the types of benchmarking relevant to each (internal and competitive benchmarking) and introduces an interesting intermediate form (organization benchmarking) which can be used for reallocations of resources between business units and bonus plan designs.

Chapter 2 is not easy, but it should be extremely rewarding. It introduces the main operations research tool: linear programming, the Volkswagen of modern benchmarking. The introduction is novel in three ways. First, unlike in existing business textbooks, linear programming is not presented as an engineering device that determines in a mechanical way how a function is optimized subject to constraints. Instead the discussion is centered on the economic concept of accounting prices. Second, the main results are derived in an elementary way. Third, I show how to do linear programming with Excel.

Chapter 3 is core. It presents the tool of data envelopment analysis. The point of departure is quite standard, a calculation of how much more output a business unit could produce if it were to adopt best practices, but the way in which accounting prices are immediately determined and used is novel. This approach paves the way for a crisp discussion of the interrelationships between the important but different concepts of efficiency, productivity, and profitability in **Chapter 4**. At this point I also discuss the econometrics of benchmarking, including an explanation of the basic ideas underlying the tool of stochastic frontier analysis.

Chapter 5 discusses the subtleties that surround the main application of benchmarking, namely ranking. It is quite a persuasive management tool that provides a sense of direction and infiltrates all corners of the information society. I keep the analysis as simple as possible by ignoring scale economies or diseconomies. Since scale effects play an important role in the practice of benchmarking I present their ramifications in **Chapter 6**.

Chapter 7 reiterates the usefulness of the economic tack to benchmarking which is outlined in this book.

Doonesbury © 2006 G.B. Trudeau.
Reprinted by permission of Universal Press Syndicate. All rights reserved.

1

WHAT IS BENCHMARKING AND WHY IS IT USEFUL?

To give an example of the difference between the *comparative* concept of efficiency and the *absolute* concept of productivity Professor Subhash Ray quoted the late comedian Henny Youngman. When asked "How is your wife?" Youngman responded, "Compared with what?"[1] Indeed, a precise answer to such a question requires a yardstick or reference point and that is not always easy to find. Moreover, there may be disagreement on what constitutes an "ideal" reference point; it may vary between cultures, businesses, or even individuals. Yet the very concept of benchmarking requires the use of reference points.

The compromise put forward in this book is that a reference point need not be *the* reference point, applicable indiscriminately to all business units or other objects we want to compare. Differ-

---

1   Subhash Ray's soundbite was at the Fifth International Symposium on Data Envelopment Analysis and Performance Management, Indian School of Business, Hyderabad (2007). Mladjenovic (2002) gives the same quote.

ent business units deserve different benchmarks to be measured up to. This raises the question: what are those benchmarks?

The basic theme of this book is that a reference point need not be preconceived, but can be the outcome of the analysis. Objects are measured—possibly in different dimensions—and we then consider the collection of all objects. We then calculate how much better an object under consideration could be if we reallocated our resources to substitutes with the same proportions of measures. One of the advantages of this methodology is that it requires no single reference point. This approach is relevant when measures are given by multiple figures, in other words when objects score in *different* dimensions.

The performance measurement literature speaks of *decision making units*. It is rather peculiar language—geared towards business analysis—but the concept is widely applicable. For Henny Youngman the "decision making unit" is a wife. More classical examples of decision making units are divisions within a corporation, supermarkets in a chain, branches of a bank, and firms within an industry. In such contexts the idea of benchmarking is simple. We conduct a thought experiment, and ask how much better a decision making unit *could* perform if it were free to adopt the practices of the other units. Here a decision making unit is treated like a machine that transforms inputs (its resources) into outputs (its scores in different dimensions). The input–output proportions (between resources and scores) are like a recipe, and constitute the practice of the decision making unit.

Let us a look at a simple example, a single output industry with three firms (see Table 1.1). One firm employs labor, another capital, and a third both. For simplicity I assume that each firm produces one unit of output, and that the specialized firms (that is, on the input side) use one unit of their respective inputs. The third firm employs l units of labor and k units of capital, where l and k are positive numbers. Could the third firm perform better? If it uses more input than firm 1 or 2, it could. Let's look at this more closely.

The only alternative for firm 3 would be to adopt the specialized practices of firms 1 and 2. Since we assumed that each of them transforms one unit of input to one unit of output, the

Table 1.1 Three firms producing the same output with different inputs

	Firm 1	Firm 2	Firm 3
Units of output	1	1	1
Units of labor input	1	0	l
Units of capital input	0	1	k

alternative mode of production would yield a hypothetical output of $l + k$. If this figure falls short of the actual output of firm 3 (one unit, by assumption), the answer is no, firm 3 cannot produce more. Hence, if $l + k < 1$, the answer is no, firm 3 cannot improve its performance. But if $l + k$ is more, say 1.1, firm 3 *can* produce more. Its output, 1, can be *expanded* by employing its resources using the practices of the other firms. The expansion factor would be 1.1, and is called *potential output*. Since firm 3 produces only 1/1.1 = 91% of its potential output, we say it is 91% efficient. The two cases ($l + k < 1$ and $l + k > 1$) are encompassed by a single formula for the so-called *expansion factor*, which is denoted by e. In our example $e = \max\{l + k, 1\}$. If $l + k < 1$, this expansion factor equals 1, confirming that the firm can do no better, and otherwise the expansion factor is $l + k$. *Efficiency* is defined as the ratio of actual output (1) to potential output (e): $1/e$. This definition extends beyond the example. If a firm could produce 25% more if it were to process its inputs using best practice techniques, it produces only 80% of its potential output (since 1 is 80% of 1.25) and we therefore say it is 80% efficient.

Instead of asking how much more firm 3 could produce given its inputs, we might ask how much less input it would need to produce its output. We shall see that this problem reformulation does not alter the measures, at least when there are no scale effects. Let me first present a simple numerical example of Table 1.1, in Table 1.2 (overleaf).

In Table 1.2, firm 3 commands a lot of input, in fact more than it needs. If it adopted the specialized techniques of firms 1 and 2 (which produce output in a one-to-one ratio from either input), output would rise to ¾ + ½ = 5/4 units. The flipside of the coin is

Table 1.2 Numerical example of three firms producing the same, single output

	Firm 1	**Firm 2**	**Firm 3**
Units of output	1	1	1
Units of labor input	1	0	¾
Units of capital input	0	1	½

that firm 3 can contract its inputs by a factor of 4/5 to produce its output.

Consider a contraction of firm 3's inputs of l units of labor and k units of capital in the slightly more general Table 1.1, by a factor $c < 1$, so that $c{\times}l$ units of labor and $c{\times}k$ units of capital remain available to firm 3. If firm 3 were to stick to its own practice, its output would fall back by the same factor below the initial output level of 1. Hence the only way it can hope to preserve its level of output is to adopt the practices of firms 1 and 2. This diversification would yield $c{\times}l$ of output using firm 1's technology plus $c{\times}k$ of output using firm 2's technology, and the total output would be the targeted quantity of 1 if $c(l + k) = 1$.

Hence the contraction factor equals $c = 1/(l + k)$. This number is a *contraction* factor, $c < 1$, only if $l + k > 1$, as is the case in Table 1.2, where $l = ¾$ and $k = ½$. Otherwise firm 3 would already be efficient and it would be unproductive to adopt the alternative practices; input contraction would not be feasible. To incorporate the qualification $l + k > 1$, the contraction factor is modified as $c = \min\{1/(l + k), 1\}$. This contraction factor happens to be the inverse of the expansion factor $e = \max\{l + k, 1\}$. And since efficiency is defined as the inverse of the expansion factor, we may conclude that efficiency can also be seen as the percentage of the inputs used that is necessary to produce the outputs.

As I have already suggested, this result holds generally provided there are *constant returns to scale*. This assumption means that it is always possible to expand (or contract) all inputs and outputs with a common factor. This is not a bad assumption in manufacturing. If you want to produce double the number of cars, you need double the number of engines, tires, and so on. In other sectors, including web-based information services, you need not double all your inputs when you want to reach double the number of customers. There are benchmarking models that do not assume constant returns to scale, but they are a little more complicated, and we shall look at them later in the book.

Our single output firms are a simplification of the real world, where firms are produce a variety of products, and moreover are assessed in terms of different criteria. Firms score in different dimensions, but only two are required to understand the principles of benchmarking. Consider an industry with two outputs. For ease of explanation I now assume there is a single input, labor. In Table 1.3, three firms each employ one worker. Firms 1 and 2 are specialized, now on the output side, with firm 1 producing one unit of good 1 and firm 2 one unit of good 2. Firm 3 produces y units of good 1 and z units of good 2.

Table 1.3 Three firms producing different outputs with the same input

	Firm 1	Firm 2	Firm 3
Units of output 1	1	0	y
Units of output 2	0	1	z
Units of labor input	1	1	1

Let us pursue the same reasoning as in the previous thought experiment, and ask how much more output firm 3 could produce. Since we do not want to add apples and oranges, we consider an expansion of both its outputs by a common factor, which we can call e again. In other words, we fix the mix of products. This procedure handles all sorts of demand conditions. It is only natural when the products are perfect complements, like whisky and soda, or hardware and software, but even if the products are substitutes, like whisky and vodka, or laptops and desktops, it is a sensible approach. By fixing the output mix we rule out expansions which make use of marketing information about customers' willingness to substitute, and therefore our estimate of potential output will be conservative. Hence we consider the hypothetical situation in which firm 3 produces not y but ey units of good 1 and not z but ez of good 2, and ask how big expansion factor e can be.

The only alternative technologies available to firm 3 are the specialized ones of firms 1 and 2. Since firms 1 and 2 are equally labor intensive and the ratio of outputs of firm 3 is y to z in Table 1.3, the best use of the specialized techniques is obtained by dividing the labor of the worker of firm 3 between $y/(y + z)$ for the production of the first output and $z/(y + z)$ for the production of the second output. Since the specialized techniques yield one unit of output per input, the outputs would be $ey = y/(y + z)$ and $ez = z/(y + z)$. Comparison with the actual outputs y and z shows that the expansion factor of firm 3 is $e = 1/(y + z)$.

This number is an *expansion* factor, $e > 1$, only if $y + z < 1$. Otherwise, i.e. if $y + z \geq 1$, firm 3 would already be efficient and it would be unproductive to adopt the alternative practices; output expansion would not be feasible. If we include the qualification $y + z < 1$, the expansion factor of firm 3 is modified as $e = \max(1/(y + z), 1)$. As before, the efficiency of firm 3 is given by the inverse expression, $1/e = 1/\max(1/(y + z), 1)$, and this can be rewritten as $e = \min(y + z, 1)$. The latter expression reveals that if firm 3's total output ($y + z$) is less than 1, then its efficiency is less than 100%, while if total output of firm 3 is equal to or more than 1, its efficiency is the full 100%.

Now let me turn to the important issue of valuations. In Table 1.3 the diversified firm produces quantities y and z of the respective outputs. If it is not efficient—producing only $y + z < 1$ of total output—the best-practice firms or *benchmarks* are the specialized firms. Since each benchmark firm transforms one unit of (labor) input into one unit of the respective outputs, the efficient production prices are 1 for each product, expressed in labor costs. Now if these production prices prevail, the diversified firm, firm 3, would operate at a loss, because revenue would be $1*y + 1*z$, cost would be 1, and the former is less than the latter. These prices are called *accounting prices*. Since they reflect the costs of the best production practices, accounting prices of outputs are knife edge, too low to sustain less than fully efficient production activities.

Benchmarking—either by determining the greatest expansion factor for the outputs given the inputs, or by determining the smallest contraction factor for the inputs given the outputs—is useful because it maps the potential of a decision making unit, quantitatively—comparing actual output with potential output—and qualitatively—by identifying the best practices that would bring about the potential output. In the last example (at least when output of the diversified firm totals less than 1), more could be produced with the technologies of the specialized firms, and therefore it would be rational to adopt these best practices. When the pool of decision making units is much larger than three, it is more difficult to identify the best practice techniques for a decision making unit, and we need the operations research technique of linear programming to spot the benchmarks, but the idea remains the same.

There is a difference between benchmarking an individual decision making unit, like Mrs. Youngman, and benchmarking all decision making units, like the population of wives. The constellation of decision making units that are each other's peers is called an *organization*. The organization could be a corporation (comprising divisions), a chain (of supermarkets), a bank (of branches), or an industry (consisting of firms). The benchmarking of an organization against other organizations is not conceptually different from the benchmarking of a decision making unit against its peers. For example, we could analyze how much better a bank could perform if it benchmarked its branches against each other, but it might also learn from measuring itself against the other players in the industry. The same linear programming tool can be used for internal benchmarking as for competitive benchmarking.

Internal benchmarking is practiced only by big organizations, which include many business units. The more units there are as a backdrop for comparisons, the greater the likelihood is that other units with a similar scope of outputs and of inputs will be available for comparison. After all, the objective of benchmarking is to "steal" production or business processes from similar, but better units. The advantages of competitive benchmarking are that we fish in a bigger pool for best practices, thus setting a higher standard, and that we can make comparisons at the company level, which includes elements not captured at the division level, such as overhead. The drawback of competitive benchmarking is, of course, the difficulty of acquiring the data.

External or competitive benchmarking is applicable both to business units and to corporations. In the former case, comparable intra-company information is required for different companies. In Table 1.4 this case is denoted by the box "Competitive benchmarking." In the latter case aggregate company data are compared, which is less demanding. This case is the box "External benchmarking" in Table 1.4.

Table 1.4 A taxonomy of benchmarking

	Reference organization	
Decision making unit	**Corporation**	**Industry**
Business unit	Internal benchmarking	Competitive benchmarking
Corporation	Organization benchmarking	External benchmarking

There is an interesting intermediate level of benchmarking, in between internal and external or competitive benchmarking. It is the benchmarking of an organization by measuring it against its own constituent parts. The idea is borrowed from economic theory, which has developed a subtle technique to measure the efficiency of an economy without comparing it with other economies. Here inefficiency encompasses not only suboptimal production of outputs by firms (excessive use of inputs), but also the subtle form of inefficiency economists call *allocative inefficiency*. All firms in an economy may produce efficiently, but the allocation of resources may be suboptimal. The same logic is applicable to a corporation. There may be scope for performance improvement by reallocating resources between business units. If so, the units may be efficient, but the organization is not. This source of inefficiency can be exposed without benchmarking the organization against its competitors, by benchmarking the organization against its own parts. If we benchmark an organization internally, a subtle conceptual issue emerges. We have to resolve the issue that benchmarks are specific to the decision making unit being considered. While internal and competitive benchmarking are the same ballgame from the point of view of technical analysis, *organization benchmarking* is distinct in that it requires some extra work.

If we simply assess the performance of a branch manager—perhaps to determine her bonus—by benchmarking her branch against all other branches, the result of our analysis will be idiosyncratic in the sense that the benchmark or benchmarks against which we measure her up must have comparable profiles of services and of resources. Different decision making units may turn out to have different benchmarks. There are two grounds for such differences. On the *output* side, branches may focus on different products: for a bank, say, perhaps mortgages or business loans. On the *input* side branches may employ different processes, such as more or fewer automated teller services, or also be not comparable in the nature of certain inputs. Air-conditioning is important in some regions and indeed may be more or less efficient, but irrelevant in others. In short, your benchmarks must be comparable in terms of the mix of outputs and the mix of inputs.

If, however, we benchmark a bank against its own branches, then we analyze the performance of the organization given the bank's *total* inputs and *total* outputs. We do so by analyzing how much better the organization could perform if not only each decision making unit operated efficiently, but also the organization's resources were allocated optimally. This problem can also be solved by the operations research technique of linear programming, but this time the benchmark valuations relate to the organization as a whole. The results are no longer specific to decision making units, and can be used to rank them objectively. More precisely, the accounting prices of the organization can be used to value the contributions of all units, *without* running into the problem that the weights in the valuation differ across firms and may influence the results. This feature renders organization benchmarking distinct. The company-wide accounting prices can be used to reallocate resources between business units and to design bonus plans.

The difference between benchmarking decision making units and the organization as a whole is subtle, because it emerges only if inputs or outputs are multi-dimensional and weights are needed to compare the performance contributions of components. In the literature this problem is often a no-brainer, because performance weights are considered to be given in the analysis, and then there is no reason indeed to change them as we benchmark one decision making unit, another, or the entire organization. In practice, however, it is not easy to assign weights to different performance components. Universities struggle to compare educational achievements with research output, business schools factor in starting salaries of their graduates, and businesses themselves juggle with not only financial targets, but also others, like customer satisfaction. How do we weigh the importance of all these different performance facets? Ultimately this is a *valuation* problem, and the determination of values is the classical problem of the science of economics. This is why the theory expounded in this book is the *economics* of benchmarking.

Paradoxically, the economic approach to benchmarking taken in this book is particularly useful for organizations that are *not* run as a traditional economic unit. The economic theory of the firm departs from the proposition that the menu of possible strategies is limited by the technological possibilities. This proposition is reflected in the modeling of strategies as combinations of inputs and outputs, a framework that encompasses many choices, like which products to produce, how much of each, when, and using which inputs in which proportions. The standard assumption of economic theory is that the prices are determined in the market place and can be used to value the benefits and costs of alternative strategies. This assumption is not innocent but it presumes that there are complete markets.

Many organizations produce services that are not traded in the market place, and therefore cannot be evaluated in financial terms, such as revenues. That does not free them from economic problems, such as cost minimization or maximizing the output of the desired services. This is where benchmarking becomes important. Pure business enterprises have the great advantage that there are natural measures for their strategies, namely the prices of the output and input components, which moreover allow for aggregation into a single aggregate: profit. Since the discounted stream of expected profits is reflected in the stock price, there is a one-dimensional score and "benchmarking" is reduced to reading stock listings in the newspaper. But other organizations, including nonprofits and various intermediate types like publicly provided services, need management tools to weigh the importance of different output and input components.

Benchmarking is such a tool, albeit indirectly. It is based on the comparison of different and possibly non-financial output and input components between decision making units, such as exam scores and teacher resources in education; overhead and outreach in charities; personnel, equipment and success rates in health care. It not only marks the relative performance of the different units, it also determines the importance of the different components. In other words, benchmarking has the capacity to put numbers on the different components of an organization's outputs and inputs. This feature is particularly helpful where markets fail to fulfil the function, as they do for nontraditional organizations, including nonprofits. It may also resolve the puzzle that benchmarking may be more widespread among semi-public organizations than purely private ones.

For the airline industry, Francis, Humphreys and Fry (2005) present the interesting information reproduced in Table 1.5.

The authors make the following observations:

When examining the performance improvement techniques used in relation to ownership, the results are not necessarily what might have been expected. There is a tendency for those airlines with a government stake in ownership to make greater use of performance improvement techniques.

Table 1.5 Performance improvement techniques used in relation to ownership

Technique	Government stake %*	No government stake %**	Total %
Benchmarking	100	78	88
Quality management systems (ISO9000/BS5750 or similar)	74	36	54
Balanced scorecard	58	32	44
Business process reengineering	53	27	39
Activity-based costing	42	27	34
Total quality management (TQM)	37	10	22
Environmental management systems (e.g. ISO14000)	32	5	17
Value-based management	16	14	15
Business excellence model/EFQM	11	5	7

*   Percentage use by airlines with a government stake in ownership.
**   Percentage use by airlines without a government stake in ownership.

Source: Francis, Humphreys and Fry (2005).

Contrary to the authors I am not surprised by the more extensive use of benchmarking in semi-government businesses. Benchmarking can be used as a performance measurement tool, which comes in handy in environments where not all objectives are monetarized by markets. In the semi-public sphere, there are typically multiple objectives, some monetarized, others not. Benchmarking can be used to value the non-monetary objectives. Moreover, even when objectives are monetarized—by price-setting semi-government organizations—it is not always clear how this should be done, and benchmarking offers some useful solutions. In short, benchmarking is an instrument that can be employed to fill the gaps where markets do not reign. This pricing role of benchmarking is little known, but I place it center stage.

The central idea of this book is to benchmark without preconceived preferences for different performance measures, and simultaneously to reveal the implicit weights. It has a slightly unusual implication for the organization of the book. Since I want to take the reader quickly to valuation issues, I have placed linear programming up front, even though it is technically the most demanding chapter.

In order not to scare you to death, I have invested quite some effort into making Chapter 2 palatable. It does not assume any mathematical knowledge, and the theory is introduced in a rather geometrical way, with what I hope you will see as slick pictures. I center the analysis on the concept of an accounting price, which will be used as the revolving door between all chapters. I realize that an accounting price is no easy concept, and suggest you take your time to read the next chapter. Once you grasp it, the fruits will be rewarding. And as a bonus you will acquire a deep insight into this branch of operations research, including its climax, the main theorem of linear programming. This theorem imputes the benefits of an efficient decision making unit or organization to the contributing inputs. Roughly speaking, the inputs are rewarded according to their scarcities. The main point of linear programming is that it determines the rewards.

At least that is my view. Most texts are different, and stress the mechanics of linear programming. While in the old days that may have been useful, nowadays any computational aspect is a piece of cake, even for grandmothers' laptops. My focus on valuation issues immediately pays off in the next chapter, where I explain the technique of benchmarking. The novelty of this approach is that it uncovers the role of preference weights in benchmarking, without the need to fix them in some preconceived manner.

Another great advantage of putting accounting prices center stage is that they facilitate a crisp discussion of some seemingly related but quintessentially different concepts, namely those of efficiency, productivity, and profitability. While the nuances may have been clear to Henny Youngman when he thought of his decision making unit, the concepts tend to be confused in business thinking. The apparatus of benchmarking explains them through a series of simple examples, and is a useful tool for performance ranking, the topics of Chapters 4 and 5. The flipside of the coin of taking the reader quickly to an accounting price framework for benchmarking is that standard, more technical modifications on the returns to scale must wait until Chapter 6.

Further reading

I shall end each chapter with suggestions for some further reading. For the traditional approach to benchmarking I recommend Camp (1989) and Bogan and English (1994). They present benchmarking as a comparison tool, and emphasize implementation issues in the organization. For the application of benchmarking to quality management I recommend Zairi (1996) and Watson (2007). The latter also provides a smorgasbord of practicalities as a taxonomy of business benchmarking, an alternative to my Table 1.4.

LINEAR PROGRAMMING IN ONE LESSON

Linear programming is the basic technique of operations research. You may have heard of it, but I want you to know what it is exactly, for benchmarking—at least when there are different score dimensions—is basically solving a simple linear program. Nowadays it is such a standard routine that linear programming is embedded in Microsoft's worksheet program, Excel®, and I shall show how it works in that context. First, however, I must present some theory, to enable you to understand what is really going on when you punch your keys.

Linear programming is the maximization or minimization of a linear function subject to linear constraints. It is enough to consider maximization, for the minimization of a function, say $f(x)$, is equivalent to the maximization of $-f(x)$. I introduce linear programming by considering a problem with two variables, the production of two goods, say hardware x_1 and software x_2, and two constraints, a labor constraint $c_{11}x_1 + c_{12}x_2 \leq b_1$ and a capital constraint $c_{21}x_1 + c_{22}x_2 \leq b_2$. The b's on the right-hand sides are the *bounds* (the available labor and capital) and the c's on the left-hand sides are the *constraint coefficients*. The first subscript of a constraint coefficient identifies the constraint, and the second the variable to which it applies. The labor and capital coefficients of hardware are c_{11} and c_{21} respectively, and of software these coefficients are c_{12} and c_{22}. For example, coefficient c_{21} denotes the amount of capital required to produce one unit of hardware. The labor/capital intensities are c_{11}/c_{21} for hardware and c_{12}/c_{22} for software. These may differ quite a bit. It will be that $\frac{c_{11}}{c_{21}} < \frac{c_{12}}{c_{22}}$, as software is more labor intensive.

In linear programming the objective is to *maximize* some linear combination of the variables, say $a_1x_1 + a_2x_2$, where the a's are the objective function coefficients. If the objective function coefficients are the prices of hardware and software, the objective would be to maximize sales revenue.

We can draw the *feasible* set, the set of all hardware-software combinations (x_1, x_2) that fulfill the constraints. It is the set of points under the two thick lines that depicts the points fulfilling the constraints with equality, $c_{11} x_1 + c_{12} x_2 = b_1$ and $c_{21} x_1 + c_{22} x_2 = b_2$. (See Figure 2.1.)

In Figure 2.1 the three thin lines are *isoquants* of equal revenue, lines where the objective function takes constant values:

$$a_1x_1 + a_2x_2 = \text{constant} \tag{1}$$

Since equation (1) can be rewritten in high-school format, with the second variable expressed explicitly as a function of the first variable, $x_2 = \text{constant}/a_2 - \frac{a_1}{a_2} x_1$, the slope of each of any of the three isoquants is $-\frac{a_1}{a_2}$. Now at the optimum, indicated by the point x^* in Figure 2.1, the value of the slope of the isoquant of the objective function must be intermediate, that is, in between the values of the slopes of the constraints:

$$\frac{c_{11}}{c_{12}} \leq \frac{a_1}{a_2} \leq \frac{c_{21}}{c_{22}} \tag{2}$$

Let me explain why the inequalities in (2) must hold. I do so "by contradiction," that is, by showing what nonsense would be

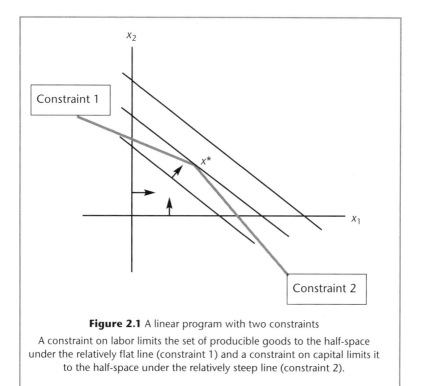

Figure 2.1 A linear program with two constraints

A constraint on labor limits the set of producible goods to the half-space under the relatively flat line (constraint 1) and a constraint on capital limits it to the half-space under the relatively steep line (constraint 2).

implied if the inequalities were violated. If the first inequality is violated—that is, $\frac{c_{11}}{c_{12}} > \frac{a_1}{a_2}$—it would pay to reduce the first variable by one unit. The reduction in x_1 would enable an increase in x_2 by $\frac{c_{11}}{c_{12}}$ (and still observe constraint 1) and alter the value of the objective function by $-a_1 + a_2\frac{c_{11}}{c_{12}}$, which is positive.[1] This improvement violates the presumed optimality of point x^*. The second inequality in (2) can be confirmed in the same way.

---

1   Strictly speaking this is positive only if a_2 is positive. Otherwise an increase in the first variable would yield an improvement.

Condition (2) lies at the heart of duality analysis, a technique that values constraints, pricing labor and capital in the present example. Before I explain this, it will be very handy to introduce a mathematical device which you may have seen before (but don't worry if you haven't). A *vector* is a string of numbers, placed in parentheses, like (2 3). The order matters: in other words, (3 2) is a different vector. Vectors summarize the orientation of straight lines. A straight line, such as that given by (1), can be represented by the vector of the coefficients: $(a_1\ a_2)$. This so-called *normal* vector is perpendicular to the straight line, as indicated in Figure 2.1.

This may need a little explanation. For example, if equation (1) reads $x_1 + x_2$ = constant, i.e. the coefficients are given by $(a_1\ a_2)$ = (1 1), then the straight line runs diagonally from northwest to southeast with slope -45° while the normal points northeast, with slope +45°, confirming they are perpendicular. The three parallel straight lines in Figure 2.1 have a lower slope, around -33°. The equation reads $0.65 \times x_1 + x_2$ = constant. The normal vector in Figure 2.1 is $(a_1\ a_2)$ = (0.65 1); since the second component is

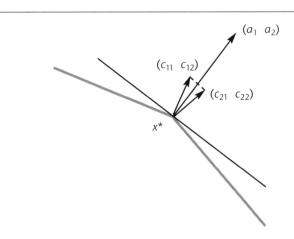

Figure 2.2 The optimum
The thick lines represent the constraints. The thin line is an isoquant of the objective function. The normal vectors of the three lines are indicated. Because the isoquant has intermediate slope, its normal vector, $(a_1\ a_2)$, resides in between the normal vectors of the constraints, $(c_{11}\ c_{12})$ and $(c_{21}\ c_{22})$.

bigger than the first it points up relative to the northeastern direction, preserving perpendicularity with the straight line.

Figure 2.1 also depicts the vectors belonging to the horizontal axis, $x_2 = 0$, which is like formula (1), but with $(a_1 \ a_2) = (0 \ 1)$, and of the vertical axis, which is like formula (1), but with $(a_1 \ a_2) = (1 \ 0)$. Figure 2.2 puts a magnifying glass on the optimum, point x^* in Figure 2.1.

Since the thin line has an intermediate slope—see formula (2)—the normal vector of this isoquant, vector $(a_1 \ a_2)$, must be in between the normal vectors of the constraints, $(c_{11} \ c_{12})$ and $(c_{21} \ c_{22})$, as depicted in Figure 2.2. It follows that vector $(a_1 \ a_2)$ must be some nonnegative combination of the latter two:

$$(a_1 \ a_2) = \lambda_1(c_{11} \ c_{12}) + \lambda_2(c_{21} \ c_{22}); \ \lambda_1, \lambda_2 \geq 0 \qquad (3)$$

Once more, this may need some explanation. If we have two vectors, such as $(c_{11} \ c_{12})$ and $(c_{21} \ c_{22})$ the nonnegative combination with weights ½, i.e. $\frac{1}{2}(c_{11} \ c_{12}) + \frac{1}{2}(c_{21} \ c_{22})$, is the mean vector which resides right in the middle. We can also take a weighted average, like ¼ $(c_{11} \ c_{12})$ + ¾ $(c_{21} \ c_{22})$. This vector is closer to vector $(c_{21} \ c_{22})$. The set of all weighted averages is given by the straight line connecting vectors $(c_{11} \ c_{12})$ and $(c_{21} \ c_{22})$: see the dashed line in Figure 2.2. If we admit weights which do not add to unity, we fill the cone spanned by vectors $(c_{11} \ c_{12})$ and $(c_{21} \ c_{22})$. The cone is the set of nonnegative combinations. Since vector $(a_1 \ a_2)$ in Figure 2.2 is between vectors $(c_{11} \ c_{12})$ and $(c_{21} \ c_{22})$, it belongs to the cone, hence is a nonnegative combination. This completes the explanation of equation (3).

Equation (3) is crucial: in fact it characterizes the optimum. The weights λ_1 and λ_2 constitute *accounting prices*, one for each constraint. Thus, λ_1 values labor and is called the *shadow wage rate*. Similarly, λ_2 values capital and is the *shadow rental rate*. The symbol λ is the Greek letter *l* and this notation honors the inventor of the analysis, the mathematician Lagrange. Shadow prices are also called *Lagrange multipliers*, particularly in computer output. The first (left) component of equation (3), namely $a_1 = \lambda_1 c_{11} + \lambda_2 c_{21}$, indicates that the price of the first good (hardware), a_1, equals the unit labor cost of hardware, $\lambda_1 c_{11}$, plus the unit capital cost of hardware, $\lambda_2 c_{21}$. The labor and capital coefficients (c_{11} and c_{21}, respectively) measure the input requirements of a unit of hardware, and are priced by λ_1 and λ_2, the accounting prices. Similarly, the second (right-hand) component of equation (3), namely $a_2 = \lambda_1 c_{12} + \lambda_2 c_{22}$, shows the cost structure of the second good, software. These two equations, the so-called *first order conditions* of the linear program, can be solved for the two accounting prices, λ_1 and λ_2.

Accounting prices express the value of outputs in terms of costs, and leave no room for profit. Accounting prices are like market prices, *if* the market is perfectly competitive and prices are driven down to cost by price competition, possibly through the entry of new firms. In perfectly competitive markets, inputs are rewarded according to their productivity and the prices of outputs are determined by the minimal costs. This link between prices and productivity gets reflected in another link, that between profit and performance. In reality, however, market prices are distorted and may reflect monopoly power, trade preferences and many other non-cost based advantages. Consequently, profit need not indicate performance. Accounting prices mimic hypothetical perfectly competitive market prices and constitute a solid foundation for benchmarking.

First we must extend the analysis to the general case, with arbitrarily many variables and constraints. Luckily, this is straightforward. If we have n variables, say x_1 through x_n, and m bounds, say b_1 through b_m, for m constraints, say $(c_{11} \ldots c_{1n})$ through $(c_{m1} \ldots c_{mn})$, the *linear program* reads:

$$\max_{x_1, \ldots x_n} a_1 x_1 + \ldots + a_n x_n : \tag{4}$$
$$c_{11} x_1 + \ldots + c_{1n} x_n \leq b_1$$
$$\vdots$$
$$c_{m1} x_1 + \ldots + c_{mn} x_n \leq b_m$$

Equation (3) becomes the so called *dual equation*:

$$(a_1 \ldots a_n) = \lambda_1 (c_{11} \ldots c_{1n}) + \ldots + \lambda_m (c_{m1} \ldots c_{mn}); \lambda_1, \ldots, \lambda_m \geq 0 \tag{5}$$

Be aware that the dual equation features coefficients, but *no* bounds! Yet the bounds do play a role. They will codetermine the numerical values of the shadow prices. More specifically, we shall see that the accounting prices relate the optimal value of the linear program, (4), to the constraining entities, the bounds. The accounting prices thus determine the distribution of the optimal value. This result is called the main theorem of linear programming, which I shall derive now. The analysis starts with the distinction between binding and nonbinding constraints.

Yes, constraints may be nonbinding. For example, if we maximize variable x subject to the constraints $x \leq 1$ and $x \leq 2$, the second constraint is clearly nonbinding. Nonbinding constraints play no role, may be ignored, and have zero accounting price:

$$c_{i1}x^*_1 + \ldots + c_{in}x^*_n < b_i \Rightarrow \lambda_i = 0 \tag{6}$$

Condition (6) is called the *phenomenon of complementary slackness*. The reason for this terminology is the following. If there is slack in a constraint, $c_{i1}x^*_1 + \ldots + c_{in}x^*_n \leq b_i$, there is no slack in nonnegativity condition $\lambda_i \geq 0$. Conversely, if there is slack in the nonnegativity condition, $\lambda_i > 0$, it cannot be that $c_{i1}x^*_1 + \ldots + c_{in}x^*_n < b_i$ (as (6) would contradict $\lambda_i > 0$), hence there is no slack in the constraint. In short, there may be slack in the constraint or in the nonnegativity condition of the associated accounting price, but not in both. This phenomenon of complementary slackness, (6), implies that the product of the slacks (in the constraint and the nonnegativity condition) must be zero:

$$\lambda_i[b_i - (c_{i1}x^*_1 + \ldots + c_{in}x^*_n)] = 0 \tag{7}$$

Equation (7) has a deep implication, namely that the total value that relates to the bounds by the accounting prices is given by
$$\lambda_1 b_i + \ldots + \lambda_m b_m = \lambda_1(c_{11}x^*_1 + \ldots + c_{1n}x^*_n) + \ldots + \lambda_m(c_{m1}x^*_1 + \ldots + c_{mn}x^*_n)$$
and by equation (5) this expression is simplified further to the equation,

$$\lambda_1 b_1 + \ldots + \lambda_m b_m = a_1 x^*_1 + \ldots + a_n x^*_n \tag{8}$$

Equation (8) is the *main theorem of linear programming*, and shows that accounting prices relate the optimal value of the linear program to the constraining entities. It can be shown that they do not vary when the bounds are perturbed a little.[2] Hence if we relax the first constraint by lifting bound b_i with one unit, we gain λ_i value on the left-hand side, and therefore on the right-hand side as well. Consequently the shadow price of this constraining entity measures its *marginal productivity*.

It is important to realize that accounting prices fulfill not an inequality, but an equality, namely (5). Inequalities, however, emerge in the case where the x variables are nonnegative, as is usually the case in business analysis. Let me explain this in detail, because many students are confused about it.

Nonnegativity constraints are special linear constraints, and therefore can be accommodated easily. Thus, a linear program with nonnegative x variables:

$$\max_{x_1,\ldots x_n} a_1 x_1 + \ldots + a_n x_n: \tag{9}$$
$$c_{11} x_1 + \ldots + c_{1n} x_n \leq b_1$$
$$\vdots$$
$$c_{m1} x_1 + \ldots + c_{mn} x_n \leq b_m$$
$$x_1,\ldots,x_n \geq 0$$

The first nonnegativity constraint can be written formally as $-x_1 + 0x_2 + \ldots + 0x_n \leq 0$. Its constraint coefficients are $(-1\ 0\ \ldots\ 0)$. Denote its shadow price by σ_1 and similarly σ_2 and so on for the other $n - 1$ nonnegativity constraints. Then dual equation (5) becomes:

$$(a_1 \ldots a_n) = \lambda_1(c_{11} \ldots c_{1n}) + \ldots + \lambda_m(c_{m1} \ldots c_{mn}) + \sigma_1(-1\ 0\ \ldots\ 0)$$
$$+ \ldots + \sigma_n(0\ 0\ \ldots\ -1);\ \lambda_1,\ldots,\lambda_m \geq 0;\ \sigma_1,\ldots,\sigma_n \geq 0 \tag{10}$$

From the first component a σ_1 is subtracted, etcetera. The σ's are the *slacks* in the dual constraints. Each component on the left-hand side is now smaller than the respective one on the right-hand side. Hence equality (10) can be rewritten as the following inequality:

---

2   See ten Raa (2006).

$$(a_1 \ldots a_n) \leq \lambda_1(c_{11} \ldots c_{1n}) + \ldots + \lambda_m(c_{m1} \ldots c_{mn}); \; \lambda_1, \ldots, \lambda_m \geq 0 \qquad (11)$$

Equation (10) is the dual equation for linear programs with nonnegative variables.

Let us return to the example of producing two goods with market prices a_1 and a_2, where we maximized revenue $a_1x_1 + a_2x_2$ subject to the labor and capital constraints $c_{11}x_1 + c_{12}x_2 \leq b_1$ and $c_{21} x_1 + c_{22} x_2 \leq b_2$. By the first component of dual equation (11), the price of good 1 is less than or equal to its factor costs. If the price is less, then by equation (10) there is slack $\sigma_1 > 0$ and by the phenomenon of complementary slackness, (6), the constraint represented by σ_1 must be binding. But since this is a simple nonnegativity constraint, it means $x^*_1 = 0$. In other words, goods that would incur a loss should not be produced. Conversely, if, for example, $x^*_2 > 0$, equation (6) yields $\sigma_2 = 0$, and therefore the price of that good (2) would be equal to its cost. It follows that accounting prices sort variables by their profitability. Accounting prices are knife edge. Only activities that break even under accounting prices should be undertaken if you want to maximize the proclaimed objective.

Now we have consumed the dry theory, it is time for an application. Linear programming is such a widespread tool, even extending well beyond business management and accounting, that it nowadays reaches every household. It is embedded in the workhorse of spreadsheets, namely Microsoft Office Excel®. I shall demonstrate its working by means of the Mickey Mouse benchmarking example in Table 2.1, which will recur in later chapters.

Table 2.1 Three firms producing different outputs with the same input

	Manager 1	Manager 2	Manager 3
Acquisition	30	20	52
Sales	25	43	19
Units of labor input	1	1	1

Three managers each perform two tasks: acquisitions and sales. Manager 1's outputs are 30 and 25, respectively, per unit of time. We want to assess how well he (or she) compares with his (or her) peers. Manager 2 produces 20 and 43 units, respectively, and the figures for manager 3 are 52 and 19. Manager 1 is sort of in between. Compared with manager 2 his acquisitions output is higher and his sales output lower; compared with manager 3 his performance is the other way round. Can manager 1 perform better? One way to answer this question is to contemplate a shift in his mix of outputs, either more acquisitions or more sales, but we rule this out, for two related reasons. First, determining the composition of the output mix may not be in his domain of competence. Second, a trade-off would be involved and it is not clear how to value acquisitions compared with sales.

Hence we shall simply assume that manager 1 must continue to produce outputs in the same proportion, 30 to 25. We shall calculate his *potential* outputs, the outputs he could produce if he adopted the best practice, which might be that of manager 2, manager 3, himself, or a combination thereof. The potential outputs shall be at least $30e$ and $25e$, respectively, where the number e measures the expansion factor. The expansion factor is at least 1, since that is feasible if the manager continues to do what he does, producing 30 and 25 units of the respective outputs.

Manager 1 may produce more, if he divides his time between continuing his own practice, copying the behavior of manager 2, and copying the behavior of manager 3. We can denote the three chunks of his reallocated labor time by θ_1, θ_2 and θ_3. These *intensities* must fulfill the *input constraint* $\theta_1 + \theta_2 + \theta_3 = 1$, the available unit of time. We shall assume constant returns to scale. Then in the first chunk of time he makes $30\theta_1$ acquisitions and $25\theta_1$ sales. (These are time proportionate reductions of his own outputs: see Table 2.1.) In the second period he makes $20\theta_2$ acquisitions and $43\theta_2$ sales: see Table 2.1 again. And the contributions of his third period are $52\theta_2$ acquisitions and $19\theta_2$ sales (using Table 2.1 again). In total, this allocation of time would produce $30\theta_1 + 20\theta_2 + 52\theta_3$ acquisitions and $25\theta_1 + 43\theta_2 + 19\theta_3$ sales.

The *output constraints* require these figures to be at least $30e$ and $25e$, respectively: $30\theta_1 + 20\theta_2 + 52\theta_3 \geq 30e$ and $25\theta_1 + 43\theta_2 + 19\theta_3 \geq 25e$.

The output constraints force manager 1 to preserve his mix of outputs as we push him to the maximum. Notice that every term in an output equation has a variable. The *bounds* of these constraints are *zero!* To avoid confusion you could shift the right-hand sides of the output constraints to the left-hand sides. The objective function we maximize is simply the expansion factor, e. We also have nonnegativity constraints for the intensities θ_1, θ_2 and θ_3. Strictly speaking variable e must be nonnegative as well, but this constraint will be fulfilled automatically, because $\theta_1 = 1$, $\theta_2 = 0$ and $\theta_3 = 0$ produces $e = 1$. (This represents the observed practice of manager 1.)

Before entering the information in an Excel worksheet, it is important to have a clear picture of the variables, the constraints, and the objective. Although it is not necessary, I recommend that you name the different variables and constraints. Excel does not seem to swallow Greek, so let us call the variables Theta1, Theta2, Theta3 and e. There are six constraints, one for the input, two for the respective outputs, and three nonnegativity constraints. We shall call the constraints Input, Output1, Output2, Theta1 +, Theta2 +, and Theta3 +, respectively. There is always one objective, and in this case it is the expansion factor, e. The nonnegativity constraints may be entered in the format $\theta_1 \geq 0$ (and likewise for intensities θ_2 and θ_3), but I recommend that the regular constraints are entered in the standard linear programming format (4) or (9), namely "formula $\leq$ bound." Otherwise the accounting prices may turn negative and that is confusing. The input constraint is already in this format, but the output constraints feature "$\geq$" and could better be rewritten, by multiplying them through by -1. This flips the inequality, as $3 \geq 2$ becomes $-3 \leq -2$. Hence I recommend entering the first output constraint in the following form: $-30\theta_1 - 20\theta_2 - 52\theta_3 + 30e \leq 0$. Since Excel will identify variables with the cells where you enter them, it is important to identify the left-hand side of a constraint with the coefficients. The coefficients of the first output constraint are **-30**, **-20**, **-52**, and **30**. These numbers are taken from the first row of Table 2.1. The first number is taken again (without the minus sign), because we are benchmarking manager 1. I have printed the numbers in bold, because I shall get back to them.

Switch on your computer and open the Excel program. There are two once-and-for-all setting changes you *might* need—be alerted when you cannot find something on your screen or receive an error message. First, activate the subroutine *Solver* by clicking the box under Tools/Add Ins. Second, restore the *system separators* for thousands and decimals by clicking the box under Tools/Options/International. I myself work on a U.S. laptop made in China for the European market. The default separators for thousand and a half are 1.000,5. Since I am used to American separators, as in 1,000.5, I changed the setting. The subroutine Solver does not like that and produces an error message.[3]

The first screen-print (Figure 2.3), shows all the information we feed the linear program with, before *Solver* solves it. (Note: my screenshots are from Excel 2003, and the screen might look slightly different if you are using a different version of Excel®.)

Let me explain how to build the screen in Figure 2.3. Strictly speaking, the first column (A) is not necessary. I have entered the names of the four variables, the six constraints, and the single objective. In the second column we enter numerical values for the four variables. Since at this stage we do not know what they will be, you are free to enter any initial value, e.g. default zeros. The four numbers that sprang to my mind were 1, 2, 3 and 4. Again, they are completely arbitrary. Excel identifies the variables with their locations in the worksheet. For example, the first variable (θ_1) is memorized as B1. Enter the initial value B1 = 1.

Now we turn to the constraints. The input constraint specifies that the time allotments of the manager to tasks 1, 2 and 3—representing the activities of himself and his peers—sum to unity at most. Enter the formula of this constraint in cell B10. In other words type the following: =B1+B2+B3. Do not forget to hit the Enter key. If you do that the number 6 will appear. Why? Because the first symbol ("=") tells Excel it is a formula, and it evaluates

---

3   I hope Microsoft buys this book, reads this, and will sort out the bug, but for the time being the setting restoration I suggest seems to work all right. Please accept the European notation in the screen prints below. To minimize the confusion I simply do not show any thousands separator (which can be suppressed), but decimals are shown as in 0,5 for one half.

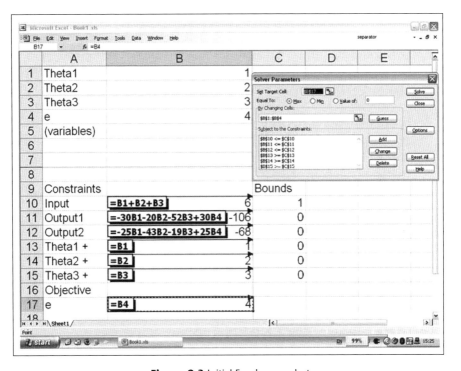

Figure 2.3 Initial Excel screenshot

Solver is prepared by entering arbitrary initial values for the variables, formulas for the constraints, values for the bounds, and specifying the objective in the worksheet. In the Solver dashboard the variables must be listed and the constraints must be specified.

formulas immediately. You cannot see the formula in the cell on the screenshot; I have added that as a comment. In the cell to the right, cell C10, enter the time bound of the input constraint (1).

Turn to the next constraint, "Output1." Remember, this constraint has zero bound, which we enter in cell C11, and the coefficients (taken from Table 2.1, with the first repeated, as we are benchmarking manager 1) are **-30**, **-20**, **-52**, and **30**. Since Excel identifies variables with the locations where we enter them, the formula for this constraint is =-30B1-20B2-52B3+30B4. When you enter this formula (don't forget the Enter key), the number -106 will pop up. That is because we have assigned the initial values 1, 2, 3, and 4. If you substitute them in the formula you get -30×1-20×2-52×3+30×4 which does indeed equal -106. The next constraint, "Output 2," is similar: see Table 2.1 and recall that we are benchmarking manager 1, so that the first coefficient recurs (without the minus sign again). I suggest the last thing you enter should be the objective: see cell B17. Leave the cursor there; in Figure 2.3 the dashed frame of cell B17 shows I did so.

Now go to Tools and click Solver. The "Solver Parameters" dashboard pops up, as in the top right-hand corner of Figure 2.3. It has set the correct "Target Cell" (because the cursor is there) and the correct operation to perform, "Max" (because it is the default). Go to the next box in the dashboard, "By Changing Cells," and enter the variables by simply clicking on the cells in the worksheet where we entered them: B1 through B4 in Figure 2.3. Next enter the first constraint, by hitting the "Add" button of the dashboard. First do the first constraint. Simply click cell B10; make sure the option ≤ is selected and enter the bound by clicking cell C10. Hit "Add" again and feed the next constraint. For the nonnegativity constraints, select the option ≥. Before you hit the magical "Solve" button, I recommend you click Solver's "Options" button and check "Assume Linear Model." This way Solver will work more efficiently and generate tailor-made output reports.

Hit the "Solve" button and two things will change on the screen: see Figure 2.4.

First and foremost, the arbitrary variable values (1, 2, 3, and 4) have been replaced by the *optimal* values in Figure 2.4. The first optimal value reads -1,10134E-13, but this is basically zero, because E-13 means 10 to the power -13, an incredibly small number. The second and third numbers are roughly one half each ($\theta_2 = 0.48$ and $\theta_3 = 0.52$). This means that if manager 1 were to work efficiently he should divide his time nearly evenly between the activities of managers 2 and 3, and not pursue his own line of activity. The fourth variable, $e = 1{,}221052632$, shows that by adopting the best practices, manager 1 could increase his output by 22%. In other words, manager 1 is not efficient.

Before you OK the Solver Results, I recommend you click the Sensitivity option under Reports, as the grey area in Figure 2.4 shows. Then clicking OK will produce a tab at the bottom for the Sensitivity Report, which takes you to Figure 2.5.

The Sensitivity Report (see Figure 2.5, overleaf) displays the

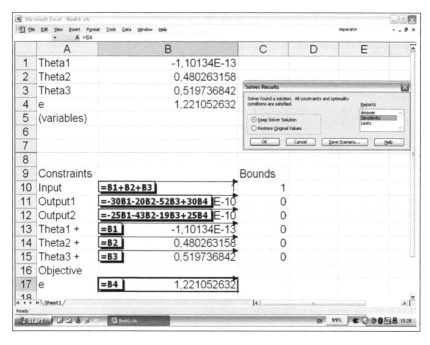

Figure 2.4 Next Excel screenshot
Solver has replaced the arbitrary initial values with the optimal ones.

following accounting prices: 1,22 for labor, 0,016 for output 1, and 0,021 for output 2.[4] This means that the second output is slightly more valuable. What does this imply? By the main theorem of linear programming the value of output is awarded to the constraining entity, labor in this example. In other words, *the value of output is equal to the resource cost.* Hence the meaning of "more valuable" is really that it is more *costly.* Here costs are defined in the economic sense as the value of the *minimally* required inputs necessary to produce the output, as determined by the best practice techniques. The best practice techniques are the ones of the benchmarks, and the latter are identified by the

---

4   I have rounded this.

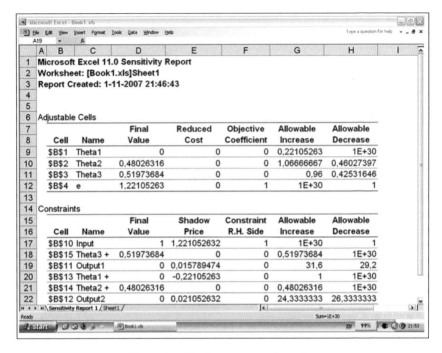

Figure 2.5 Shadow or accounting prices
Each constraint has a shadow price.

linear program. In this case Figure 2.4 reveals that the practices represented by managers 2 and 3 are run with positive intensity ($\theta_2 = 0.48$ and $\theta_3 = 0.52$). These two benchmarks codetermine the cost structure of the outputs. I shall discuss the role of accounting prices in the remainder of this book.

If you have been able to follow me through all these steps behind your computer, congratulations: you have mastered the basic tool of benchmarking and may call yourself a benchmarking novice. For further reading please refer to Chapter 4 of my (2006) text on input–output analysis and the references given there.

THE TECHNIQUE OF BENCHMARKING

In my admittedly narrow view, benchmarking is an application of linear programming, geared towards the aggregation of different scores in a single performance measure. As in the more common and wider understanding of the concept, the aim of benchmarking remains to compare a decision making unit with its peers. The classical example of a decision making unit is a firm, and the family of peers is the industry it belongs to, but many more situations are conceivable. Decision making units can be divisions of an enterprise, supermarkets forming a chain, or branches of a bank. The backdrop against which we measure up a decision making unit (the industry, the chain, or the bank) I refer to as an organization.

Formally, an *organization* consists of I *decision making units*. Decision making unit i (where $i = 1, ..., I$) is a black box that transforms *input* quantities $x^i_1,...,x^i_k$ into *output* quantities $y^i_1,...,y^i_l$. Here subscript k is the number of inputs and subscript l is the number of outputs. Superscript i indicates the decision making unit of which we take the data.

The framework is quite general, capable of encompassing many situations. For example, some commodities may be specific to a decision making unit. If decision making unit 1 is the exclusive producer of commodity 1, then y^i_1 will be zero for $i = 2, ..., I$. Nonetheless, benchmarking separates input and output classifications from decision making unit separations. In other words, some commonality of inputs and outputs must be present. If decision making units have no overlap in terms of inputs and in terms of outputs, there is no basis for comparison or benchmarking.

Although benchmarking accommodates idiosyncratic inputs and outputs, this possibility is often ignored. For better or for worse, managers pay more attention to performance scores that are uniformly applicable to different decision making units. The evidence is strong. A prominent management tool, the Balanced Scorecard of Kaplan and Norton (2005), measures business performance in four dimensions: first, financial; second, customer satisfaction; third, internal business processes (e.g. speed); and fourth, learning and growth (such as employees' morale). Every dimension may include a number of measures, some general, applicable to all similar decision making units, and some designed specifically for individual units.

To analyze the role of general and specific measures in decision making, Gascho Lipe and Salterio (2000) designed and conducted an experiment. MBA students had to evaluate two divisions of a clothing firm. The two divisions sold to different markets and had different business strategies. They had balanced scorecards with some common and some unique measures. The results showed that the experimental participants evaluated the divisions based solely on the common measures. Performance on unique measures had no effect on the evaluation judgments.

We are all prepared for the formal analysis. Focus attention on a single decision making unit, say decision making unit 1. (There is nothing special about this focus; in particular, there is no reason that the first listed decision making unit should be the biggest or the best.) We want to know at what level unit 1 operates compared with its full potential. In other words, we pose the question, how much more *could* unit 1 deliver? To answer this question we conduct a thought experiment.

We allow decision making unit 1 to redistribute its inputs over the activities represented by the inputs and outputs of all decision making units i (including itself, $i = 1$). Hence imagine that decision making unit 1 employs its inputs to run the activities of decision making units i with *intensities* θ_i, where i runs from 1 to I, the total number of decision making units. For example, if $\theta_i = 1$, decision making unit 1 would copy decision making unit i. If it is ½, it would operate decision making unit i's technology at half scale; if it is 1.1, it would reproduce decision making unit i at even a slightly higher scale than decision making unit i itself. Altogether, decision making unit 1 would need quantities $x^1_1\theta_1+...+x^I_1\theta_I$ of input 1, similar amounts of the other inputs, including amounts $x^1_k\theta_1+...+x^I_k\theta_I$ of the last input, k. With the intensities θ_i, decision making unit 1 would produce quantities $y^1_1\theta_1+...+y^I_1\theta_I$ of output 1, and so on, up to amounts $y^1_l\theta_1+...+y^I_l\theta_I$ of output l.

The envisaged operation is feasible if the required inputs do not exceed decision making unit's 1 available inputs. The operation improves the output level of decision making unit 1 if the hypothetical outputs exceed some multiple of the respective actual outputs of decision making unit 1. This output multiple is modeled by means of the so called *expansion* factor, e. The maximum expansion of output of decision making unit 1 is determined by the following linear program:

$$\max_{\theta_1,...,\theta_I,e\geq 0} e: \tag{12}$$
$$x^1_1\theta_1 +...+ x^I_1\theta_I \leq x^1_1, ..., x^1_k\theta_1 +...+ x^I_k\theta_I \leq x^1_k$$
$$y^1_1\theta_1 +...+ y^I_1\theta_I \geq y^1_1 e, ..., y^1_l\theta_1+...+ y^I_l\theta_I \geq y^1_l e$$

In program (12) the expansion factor is maximized subject to the feasibility constraints on the inputs and proportionate expansion of the outputs. *All* that is needed to run benchmarking program (12) are the inputs and the outputs of the decision making units, $x^i_1,...,x^i_k$ and $y^i_1,...,y^i_l$. respectively, for the various decision making units, i. The program can be solved using Excel's Solver, as detailed in Chapter 2, or any other linear programming routine.

Implicitly, program (12) assumes constant returns to scale. Here is the formal explanation of a simple way to understand this. Imagine we replace the input and output data of some decision making unit, let us say the last decision making unit, I, by multiplying them by t-times their current value. If $t = 1.2$ we replace decision making unit I by a 20 per cent bigger unit; if $t = 0.7$, by a 30 per cent smaller unit. In linear program (12), the coefficients of $\theta_I - x^I{}_1,...,x^I{}_k$ and $y^I{}_1,...,y^I{}_l$—would be replaced by their t-folds: $tx^I{}_1,...,tx^I{}_k$ and $ty^I{}_1,...,ty^I{}_l$. The only effect of this replacement on the solution variables of program (12) would be that θ_I is replaced by θ_I/t. If we can maximize output by running the activities at intensities θ_i and inflating the inputs and outputs of one activity with a factor t, which is essentially the same transformer of inputs to outputs (running the inflated activity at intensity θ_I/t), there are no scale effects in the model. In Chapter 6 we shall analyze more complicated models, which do not feature constant returns to scale.

The assumption of constant returns to scale enables us to normalize the activities. For example, if there are two inputs and one output, it is natural to rescale such that the outputs of all activities are equal to 1. After this rescaling decision making units differ in their inputs only, and we can plot a scatter diagram in input space: see Figure 3.1.

In Figure 3.1, decision making unit 4 can reduce its distance to the origin from 100% to 75%. That way it moves to the midpoint between decision making units 3 and 5. Indeed, if we run activities 3 and 5 at intensities ½ each, the required inputs are the average of the inputs of decision making units 3 and 5, which is represented by the midpoint, while the output would be ½ + ½ = 1, so it is unchanged. This way decision making unit 4 can produce its output using only 75% of its inputs. The remainder, 25% of the inputs, can be considered wasted (and be reallocated without reducing output). Because of the constant returns to scale assumption, the capacity to produce output with three-quarters of the inputs is equivalent to the capacity to produce four-thirds of the output with the given input. The application of program (12) to unit 4 yields an expansion factor $e = 4/3$.

Decision making unit 2, also shown in Figure 3.1, would need only some 80% of its inputs if it employed the techniques of decision making units 1 and 3; 20% of its input can be considered waste for this decision making unit. The application of program (12) to unit 2 yields an expansion factor $e = 5/4$. The lower envelope of the observations, the thick lines connecting decision

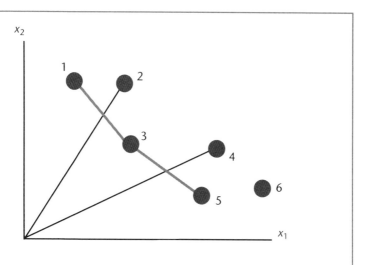

Figure 3.1 An organization with two inputs and a single output
Decision making units 1, 3, and 5 use little input. Decision making units 2, 4, and 6 can contract their inputs.

making units 1, 3, and 5, represents the minimally required inputs for the production of one unit of output. These three units are the *benchmarks*. The distance between the envelope and a decision making unit measures the unnecessary input, or inefficiency. This technique is called *data envelopment analysis* (DEA).

In general it is impossible to identify an all-purpose best practice or practices. It depends on the unit you benchmark. For example, in Figure 3.1 there is *no* general purpose best practice. For decision making unit 4 the benchmarks are decision making units 3 and 5, but for decision making unit 2 the benchmarks are decision making units 1 and 3. Basically, the relevant best practices must be compatible with the mix of resources of the unit you investigate. In Figure 3.1, decision making unit 4 is well endowed with the first input. The technique of decision making unit 1, though efficient, requires a lot of the other input, and therefore it is not relevant to decision making unit 4.[1]

---

1   In Figure 3.1 unit 6 has only one benchmark, namely unit 5.

Case study 1: Spanish restaurants

The central management of a Spanish fast-food chain of 54 restaurants wanted to reallocate resources to the managers of the more efficient restaurants, and called Giménez-García, Martínez-Parra and Buffa (2007) to organize an internal database. The outputs factors of the fast-food chain include first, sales, and second, a quality index for each restaurant unit based on quality questionnaires filled out by customers, internal service quality audits, and data provided by mystery shoppers. The only input factor that could be reallocated among the restaurant units was the total number of waiting and kitchen staff, who are interchangeable. There are also non-reallocable input factors, namely the number of seats and the number of server counters, both of which provide information about the size and serving capacity of each unit, but these "variables" are fixed in the analysis. Giménez-García and colleagues (2007) found that more than half the restaurants were not efficient, and determined the excess staff for each.

Central management imposed some further constraints on the reallocations, and the authors determined an optimal reallocation by maximizing the sum of the expansion factors of the recipient, efficient restaurants, subject to an input and an output constraint for each restaurant as in DEA program (12): with, however, additions to the input bounds, subject to the reallocation constraints. Six full-time-equivalent staff were moved. Then the DEA model was rerun for every restaurant with the new inputs to determine the newly achievable expansion factors, which central management set as output targets. The results showed that originally efficient restaurants could improve their output by an average of 4.20 percent after the reallocation of inputs, and that this reallocation was beneficial for the entire restaurant chain. The output targets were used to design bonus plans.

Let me move from the example depicted in Figure 3.1—where two inputs are combined to produce a single output—to the mirror image. Hence consider the example where one input, say labor, can be used to produce two outputs, such as serving meals and cleaning tables. In this case it is natural to exploit the assumption of constant returns to scale to the activities, such that all inputs are equal to one. Upon this rescaling decision making units differ in their outputs only, and we can plot a scatter diagram in *output* space, as depicted in Figure 3.2.

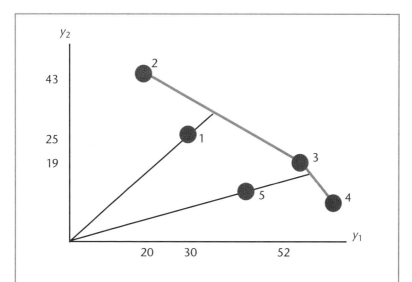

Figure 3.2 An organization with a single input and two outputs
Decision making units 2, 3, and 4 have a high output. Decision making units 1 and 5 can expand their outputs.

In output space the most efficient decision making units are on the northeastern frontier. We can envelope the data again, but now from above. If decision making unit 1 were to divide its input between the techniques employed by decision making units 2 and 3, it could produce their average output, which is represented by the midpoint. This way decision making unit 2 can expand its output by some 20%. In fact, in Figure 3.2 the output coordinates of decision making units 1 (30, 25), 2 (20, 43) and 3 (52, 19) are precisely the data of the manager's outputs of Table 2.1, which we analyzed using Excel in Chapter 2. Hence the precise output expansion figure is 22% (see Chapter 2, Figure 2.4). Figure 3.2 also shows that decision making unit 5 can produce more by adopting the techniques of decision making units 3 and 4.

Now we have developed some intuition into what is going on when we calculate wasted inputs, we can proceed with our formal analysis, to pave the way for the determination of the accounting prices, a key tool in the economic analysis of benchmarking. Accounting prices are associated with constraints. Now linear program (12) features $k + l$ ordinary constraints (k for the inputs and l for the outputs) plus I nonnegativity constraints (for the intensities with which the activities are run). Constraints are characterized by the coefficients of the variables. The variables in program (12) are the intensities θ_1, ..., θ_I and expansion factor e. Remember, the input quantities and output quantities ($i = 1, ..., I$) are *not* variables, but given, fixed data. Formally, they are *coefficients* in program (12) and also, in case of the inputs ($x^i_1,...,x^i_k$), *bounds*.

Multiplying through the output constraints in (12) by -1, to write them in standard linear programming format (with $\leq$), the coefficients in the input constraints are ($x^1_1 ... x^I_1$ 0),..., ($x^1_k ... x^I_k$ 0) and the coefficients in the output constraints are ($-y^1_1 ... -y^I_1$ y^1_1),..., ($-y^1_l ... -y^I_l$ y^1_l), where the last components reflect the right-hand sides of the second line of inequalities in program (12). These right-hand side output terms are products of outputs (coefficients) and the expansion variable. They are *not* bounds! The output constraints have no bounds; formally they are zero. The objective functions coefficients of the variables (θ_1, ..., θ_I and e) are (0 ... 0 1), since the intensities θ are tools and only the last variable feeds the objective function. This sums up the formal structure of benchmarking program (12), and we are ready to invoke the accounting prices.

Instead of using shadow prices λ's, it is customary to denote the accounting prices of the inputs by w_1, ..., w_k and of the outputs by p_1, ..., p_l. Thus, Chapter 2's dual equation (11) becomes:

$$(0 \ \ldots \ 0 \ 1) \leq w_1(x^1_1 \ \ldots \ x^I_1 \ 0) + \ldots + w_k(x^1_k \ \ldots \ x^I_k \ 0)$$
$$+ p_1(-y^1_1 \ \ldots \ -y^I_1 \ y^1_1) + \ldots + p_l(-y^1_l \ \ldots \ -y^I_l \ y^1_l); \tag{13}$$
$$w_1,\ldots,w_k \geq 0 \quad p_1,\ldots,p_l \geq 0$$

One of the inequalities in (13) is in fact an equality, as I shall argue now. The optimal value of expansion factor e is at least 1, as is seen by the following choice of the intensity variables: $\theta_1 = 1$ and $\theta_2 = \ldots = \theta_l = 0$; this amounts to a simple reproduction of decision making unit 1 itself. Hence the nonnegativity constraint for the last variable, e, is nonbinding. The phenomenon of complementary slackness, (6), yields that the slack in the dual constraint is zero. Since this is the last component in (13), we obtain the following condition:

$$p_1 y^1_1 + \ldots + p_l y^1_l = 1 \tag{14}$$

Equation (14) is the so-called price normalization constraint. It resolves arbitrariness in the program that maximizes output, (12), as I shall now explain. It has to do with the units of measurements. Imagine that all outputs are in kilograms but are to be rescaled in metric pounds. Since there are two metric pounds to the kilogram, this would double all y's. The optimal x's would not be affected, nor the relative accounting prices of either the inputs or the outputs. By equation (14) all the output prices would be halved, precisely as we expect when the unit of measurement is halved. This concludes the explanation of equation (14).

The other components of dual equation (13) read as follows:

$$p_1 y^1_1 + \ldots + p_l y^1_l \leq w_1 x^1_1 + \ldots + w_k x^1_k, \ldots, p_1 y^I_1 + \ldots + p_l y^I_l \leq w_1 x^I_1 + \ldots + w_k x^I_k \tag{15}$$

Dual inequality (15) highlights an important fact: *Accounting prices render all activities unprofitable or zero.* The distinction between negative and zero accounting profits is crucial. It signals which activities are undertaken with positive intensity: in other words, which are the benchmarks. It is easy to confirm. By the phenomenon of complementary slackness—see equation (6) in Chapter 2—we know that if an activity is run with positive intensity, $\theta^*_i > 0$, then there is no slack in the dual constraint, $p_1 y^i_1 + ... + p_l y^i_l \leq w_1 x^i_1 + ... + w_k x^i_k$, and therefore such activities must break even.

It should be mentioned that the nonpositivity of accounting profits in formula (15) is valid because of the assumption of constant returns to scale. Later in the book we shall relax this assumption and show that positive profits become possible.

Since accounting prices are shadow prices, we can invoke the marginal productivity interpretation given in Chapter 2—see formula (8) and the ensuing discussion. In the present context an input price measures by how much the output level could be raised if an additional unit of that input were available, and an output price measures how much the overall output *level* could be raised if a unit of that output were gifted. The latter argument is subtle, because in benchmarking we fix the proportions of the outputs. Hence, if a unit of some output arrives as a gift, the resources must be slightly reallocated away from the production of this output, producing a little more of the other outputs, in order to preserve the proportions. If a price of an output component is higher than of some other, it means that one unit releases more productive resources. *Output accounting prices measure their values in terms of resource costs.*

There is an interesting situation when the optimization of the output level of the decision making unit that is being considered (in our case unit 1) implies that the decision making unit itself would break even under accounting prices, such that $p_1 y^1_1 + ... + p_l y^1_l = w_1 x^1_1 + ... + w_k x^1_k$. Now by the price normalization constraint, (14), we have $w_1 x^1_1 + ... + w_k x^1_k = 1$. This happens to be the value of the bounds in linear program (12). (The items on the right-hand side of the output constraints, $y^1_1 e$ through $y^1_l e$, are not bounds, but variable terms.) By the main theorem of linear programming—see equation (8) in Chapter 2—this value equals the optimal expansion factor, e^*. In short, $e^* = 1$. This value means that decision making unit 1 cannot expand by using the techniques of other decision making units. Decision making unit 1 is its own benchmark; it is a leader.

In general, however, accounting prices make decision making units *other* than themselves break even. It is extremely interesting to identify them, because they constitute the best available practices. So we need to focus on the decision making units i for which the associated equations in (15) are binding. It constitutes the set of activities that would be run if the resources available to decision making unit 1 are used optimally, to maximize the output of unit 1.

The definition of efficiency is straightforward. Compare a decision making unit with its peers in the organization. More precisely, calculate how much more it could produce by solving program (12). Let the expansion factor be e. For example, if $e = 1.1$, it could produce 10% more, and therefore it is currently producing only $1/e = 0.91$ of its potential output. Hence *efficiency* is simply defined by the inverse value of the expansion factor of benchmarking program (12), $1/e$.

Since the expansion factor is at least 1, it follows by sheer arithmetic that *efficiency is a measure between 0 and 1*. Full efficiency ($1/e = 1$) represents the situation where a decision making unit cannot improve its performance, and so is a leader.

Case study 2: Indian banks

Debasish (2006) analyzed 93 Indian banks over the period 1997–2004. They have nine inputs: deposits received (balance sheet items), liabilities (working funds and other), labor, capital related inputs (office maintenance and supplies), operating expenses, fixed assets, borrowings, net worth, and nonperforming assets. These are used to yield seven outputs: loans, investments, profits, interest, commissions, short-term securities, and net-interest-margin. It is indeed possible to treat cost components as inputs and whatever achievement components there are as outputs, but I prefer to limit the analysis to producible outputs, which can be priced. To get some insights into the efficiency scores of the 93 banks, they are classified by size (small, medium, large), ownership (public, private, foreign) and age (young, old). Don't forget: *all* you need are the inputs and the outputs for every decision making unit to run the program.

The efficiency of smaller banks declined from 0.82 in 1998 to 0.63 in 2004. The average efficiency of medium banks did not show any consistent downward or upward trend, and the range was between 0.52 and 0.62. Larger banks showed a complete reverse trend, with their peak efficiency of 0.86 in the last year (2004) and a steady increase in efficiency from 1998 to 2004. Public sector banks were the least efficient, with values in the range from 0.44 to 0.54. Foreign banks were found to be more efficient than private banks for most of the years. New banks were found to be more efficient than old banks.

We can now use our apparatus to develop a good alternative expression for efficiency, highlighting the performance of a decision making unit we are interested in. The main tool is the main theorem of linear programming—Chapter 2's formula (8)—which equates the value of the objective function with the value of the bounds. In benchmarking the objective function is the expansion factor, e: see program (12). As noted, the value of the bounds in this program is $w_1 x^1_1 + \ldots + w_k x^1_k$. Invoking the price normalization constraint, equation (14), we conclude that the expansion factor is equal to the accounting cost/revenue ratio:

$$e = (w_1 x^1_1 + \ldots + w_k x^1_k) / (p_1 y^1_1 + \ldots + p_l y^1_l) \qquad (16)$$

Formula (16) renders the expansion factor robust with respect to price level changes. For example, halving all prices (as in the transition from kilograms to metric pounds) does not affect expression (16), because halving the numerator and halving the denominator cancel each other out. Formula (16) is important, because it weighs the importance of the inputs and the outputs for efficiency. Obviously, efficiency is increased by reducing inputs or increasing outputs. An input reduction by a unit is more effective if the shadow price is higher, and the same holds for an output increase.

A simple application is the Excel analysis of the three managers in Chapter 2: see Table 2.1. Like the others, manager 1 had only a single input, his unit of labor time. Hence formula (16), using price normalization (14), reads $e = w_1$. This is confirmed by the report in Figure 2.5 (Chapter 2), where the accounting price of the manager's input listed under "Shadow Price" of "Input" is exactly equal to the value of expansion factor e under "Final Value."

Since efficiency has been defined as the inverse of the expansion factor, equation (16) implies:

$$efficiency = (p_1 y^1_1 + ... + p_l y^1_l) / (w_1 x^1_1 + ... + w_k x^1_k) \qquad (17)$$

In words, the performance of a decision making unit is measured by the *revenue/cost ratio* at accounting prices. Georgescu-Roegen (1951) called it return to the dollar in a more complicated framework, involving investment. If performance expression (17) equals 1, the decision making unit is its own benchmark. Otherwise it could improve its performance by adoption of the practices of other units, which perform fully efficiently. Indeed, if for some other unit i it holds that $(p_1 y^i_1 + p_l y^i_l) / (w_1 x^i_1 + ... + w_k x^i_k) = 1$, then $p_1 y^i_1 + p_l y^i_l = w_1 x^i_1 + ... + w_k x^i_k$, hence there is no slack in the dual constraints (15), and—by Chapter 2's phenomenon of complementary slackness (6)—we have delineated the practices that would be run with positive intensity to achieve potential output: in other words, the benchmarks.

Equation (17) admits a frequently used interpretation of efficiency measurement. Imagine the outputs, $y^1_1, ..., y^1_l$, are produced not with the observed inputs, $x^1_1, ..., x^1_k$, but by a hypothetical, efficient decision making unit. In fact the efficient inputs are given by the solution of program (12), $x^1_1 \theta_1 + ... + x^l_1 \theta_l, ..., x^1_k \theta_1 + ... + x^l_k \theta_l$, if the outputs are inflated by expansion factor e, hence a fraction $1/e$ of these inputs is enough to produce $y^1_1, ..., y^1_l$. The efficiency of the hypothetical decision making unit is 1. Applying formula (17) to the hypothetical unit, we see that it would break even: revenue equals cost. Here 'cost' is the value of the minimally required inputs to produce the outputs, $y^1_1, ..., y^1_l$. Substituting this back in the original formula (17), as applied to decision making unit 1, we come to the following intuitive, yet powerful statement:

efficiency is the cost/value ratio of inputs. Here 'cost' is the value of the *minimally* required inputs, 'value' refers to the *actual* inputs, and *both* types of inputs are valued at accounting prices.

Before putting the theory to action, let us recap. The point of departure was the input quantities $x^i_1,...,x^i_k$ and output quantities $y^i_1,...,y^i_l$ of decision making units $i = 1, ..., I$. No more and no less! In particular, we used *no* price information. All relevant prices are generated by the process of benchmarking. For each decision making unit i we calculated how much more it could produce if it reallocated its inputs among the techniques used by all decision making units, including itself. More precisely, a linear program was used to calculate the expansion factor for its outputs. The inverse of this expansion factor measured efficiency. Indeed, if output could be expanded a lot, the unit must be inefficient. The linear program generated accounting prices for all the inputs and outputs. These prices are knife edge. Alternative practices which the linear program uses to maximally expand output break even, and practices that are not undertaken would be unprofitable. Last but not least we have shown that efficiency equals the revenue/cost ratio evaluated at the accounting prices.

The accounting prices generated by benchmarking are not necessarily equal to the market prices; in fact the differences are very useful for analysis. Unlike market prices, accounting prices are specific to the decision unit that is benchmarked. In the last figure, Figure 3.2, manager 1's benchmarks were managers 2 and 3. The benchmarking was carried out in Chapter 2, where Figure 2.5 shows that the accounting prices are 0.016 and 0.021 for the two outputs. If instead we had assessed the performance of manager 5, the benchmarks would have been managers 3 and 4. All numbers would be different, the data as well as the Excel-generated accounting prices, illustrating that accounting prices are internal and vary across decision making units.

It is possible to compare accounting prices between decision making units, without rerunning the Solver routine. Remember that accounting prices make benchmarks break even. Since all benchmarks in Figure 3.2 were rescaled such that they had one unit of input, the zero profit condition implies that revenues of benchmarks must be equal. In the first case, where we benchmarked manager 1 against managers 2 and 3, this means that the straight line through the points 2 and 3 in Figure 3.2 represents points of equal value. Now if we make the step from point 2 down to point 3, we swap 43 – 19 = 24 units of output 2 against 52 – 20 = 32 units of output 1. This means that output 2 must be relatively expensive, with an accounting price ratio of 32/24 = 4/3 = 1.33. The true accounting prices, 0.016 and 0.021, are indeed in this proportion![2] In the second case, assessing manager 5, the benchmarks are managers 3 and 4, Figure 3.2 shows that the output trade-off swapping between benchmark points 3 and 4 is simply 1 to 1. Output 2 is no longer relatively expensive.

Case study 3: Korean quality management

A very interesting application is by Yoo (1993), who uses the accounting prices across Korean companies to provide some interesting managerial insights. He analyzes total quality management, which is considered as a system with input and output processes. The inputs are leadership and organization for quality; new product development; process management; human resources management; and customer satisfaction management. And the outputs are quality improvement level compared with domestic companies, and quality improvement level compared with foreign companies.

The relative ratio of shadow prices among inputs is 10 : 3 : 2 : 1 : 3, and between outputs it is 6 : 29, for the whole sample. However, certification by the International Standards Organization (ISO) makes a difference. Firms with ISO certification have the same pattern of accounting prices, but for firms without ISO certification the ratios are different, namely 6 : 6 : 5 : 1 : 3 for the inputs and 10 : 26 for the outputs. These results show that for firms with-

---

2   This becomes very clear if we do not round. Chapter 2, Figure 2.5 shows that the accounting prices are 0.015789474 and 0.021052632. Their ratio is 1.33333333.

out ISO certification the second and third inputs are relatively important, i.e. new product development and process management. On the output side the results show that without ISO certification quality improvement compared with *domestic* companies is relatively more important than with ISO certification.

The variation in accounting prices can be used to analyze the competitiveness of an industry. If an industry is perfectly competitive, then market prices have the properties of accounting prices (with good firms just breaking even and bad firms making losses if they are active), and therefore there is no room for differences between firm accounting prices. The reason is that accounting prices are equal to marginal productivities.[3] If the marginal productivity of say labor differs between firms, the more productive firms would outcompete the less productive. Another way to understand this mechanism is to imagine that one worker moves from a less to a more productive firm. She adds more value. This creates profit potential, which in a perfectly competitive market dissipates through output price reductions, and in turn renders the less productive firm unprofitable.

Case study 4: Austrian banking deregulation

In the 1990s Austria deregulated its banking industry, further exposing banks to competitive pressures. Ali and Gstach (2000) traced the operational adjustments of 216 Austrian banks (which represent 82 percent of all Austrian banks in terms of gross total assets) to price competition. Since individual price information—

---

3   See Chapter 2, formula (8) and the ensuing discussion.

that is, by bank—was not available, they calculated and analyzed the accounting prices between 1990 and 1997, distinguishing five inputs and five outputs. The inputs were labor, physical capital, interbank deposits, purchased funds, and equity; the outputs were customer deposits, interbank loans, small loans, large loans, and securities.

The authors' point of departure was that "Improved competitiveness can be observed via a decrease in the spread of prices of inputs and outputs for banks" (Ali and Gstach 2000, p. 277). This view was confirmed by their results. The spread of prices of input variables decreased, for all but the input purchased funds for rural credit unions. The authors concluded that in response to increased competitive pressure, an expected restructuring of the input side of business was effected by management of Austrian banks. The exception for the purchased inputs of the rural credit unions was considered to be indicative of the failure of these typically very small banks as yet to adapt to the deregulated operating environment.

These observations complete "Benchmarking in a nutshell." You are sufficiently well equipped to understand and appreciate different performance measures in the further chapters.

Further reading

For further reading on DEA I recommend Ray's (2004) text. More advanced texts are referenced in the next chapters.

4

EFFICIENCY, PRODUCTIVITY, AND PROFITABILITY

Having mastered the technique of benchmarking to determine the efficiency of decision making units, we are now equipped to discuss and distinguish some important business concepts which tend to be confused. Just one example from the literature is given in this quote from Anja Yli-Viikari and colleagues (2002, p. 20), discussing farming enterprises in Finland:

> To guarantee the continuation of the production the enterprises have to be profitable. The prerequisite of the profitability is efficiency.

Now particularly in agriculture there is *no* simple connection between profitability and efficiency. The breakdown of the relationship goes both ways. On one hand, many inefficient farms are quite profitable, because prices are maintained at artificially high levels. On the other, efficient firms are not necessarily the most profitable ones. *One* way to boost profit is to cut costs, but there are many other ways, including the exercise of monopoly power to deter more efficient firms and to enjoy rents. As J. R. Hicks (1935, p. 8) quipped, "The best of all monopoly profits is a quiet life." In other words, profit need not signal efficiency!

Although there are interrelations between efficiency, productivity, and profitability—and we shall discuss them—the concepts are fundamentally *different*. I shall explain the subtleties by means of a very simple example. It features a single input–single output industry with only two firms (in other words, a duopoly). As usual, I denote the input quantities by x and the output quantities by y. I shall use w and p for the prices of the input (the labor wage) and the output (the product price) respectively, and superscripts to identify the firms, firm 1 or firm 2.

In our discussion we must distinguish market prices from accounting prices. Market prices are observed and may vary. Some firms negotiate tighter labor conditions than others; and some firms may have shrewder salespeople, who extract higher prices. A well-cited example is someone who "could sell sand to the Arabs." Indeed, in this situation any price above 0 represents sheer market power.

I denote market prices by an underscore, and reserve the regular symbols for accounting prices. In short, the symbols for firm 1 are input and output *quantities* x^1 and y^1, input and output *market prices* $\underline{w}^1$ and $\underline{p}^1$, and input and output *accounting prices* w^1 and p^1. The symbols for firm 2 are similar, but with superscript 1 replaced by superscript 2. My point of departure for discussion of the issues of efficiency, productivity, and profitability is a simple question: *Which firm performs best?* We could answer this question by solving the linear programs that benchmark a firm on the industry, one program for each firm, but for this single input–single output example that would be overkill, and we can proceed in a much simpler way.

The techniques implicit in the firm input–output observations (x^1, y^1) and (x^2, y^2) are given by the output/input ratios y^1/x^1 and y^2/x^2. These numbers give the amount of output we can produce with a unit of input, and therefore constitute the *productivities* of the respective firms. The concept of productivity gets a bit more involved in the presence of multiple inputs and outputs, but this issue can wait. In our simple duopoly, let the first firm be the more productive than the second: $y^1/x^1 > y^2/x^2$. (As a matter of fact, this is an innocent assumption, because we are free to relabel the firms; in other words we can swap their names if the inequality is the other way.) Then firm 1 can produce no more than it currently produces, at least under the assumption that the data represent all conceivable practices of production. (The assumption that all possible practices are observed is quite strong, and will be dropped in the next chapter, where we discuss stochastic frontier analysis.) Firm 2, however, could perform better by adopting the technology of firm 1. That way it would produce y^1/x^1 units per unit of input and since it commands x^2 inputs, its potential output is $(y^1/x^1) x^2$. By the presumed productivity inequality this exceeds the actually produced quantity y^2.

The expansion factor, e, measures how much firm 2 could produce relative to what it produces; it equals $e = (y^1/x^1) x^2 / y^2$. Now, as we have seen in Chapter 3, efficiency is the inverse expansion factor, measuring the actual output as a fraction of potential output: $1/e = y^2 / (y^1/x^1) x^2 = (y^2/x^2)/(y^1/x^1)$. Since firm 1 can do no better than using its own technology, its expansion factor equals 1, and therefore its efficiency is also $1 = (y^1/x^1)/(y^1/x^1)$, to present it in the same format as for firm 2. For both firms we thus have the following result: *Efficiency equals relative productivity*. Here productivity is taken relative to the best practice; indeed, firm 1's productivity features in either denominator.

A further, interesting relationship between the concepts of productivity and efficiency is established in a dynamic setting, where we track the measures through time. If we proceed to the next year, all quantities will be different. Let us assume that the changes are slight, so that firm 1 remains the productivity leader. Imagine that firm 2 has become more efficient. What does it mean? That management does a better job, producing more output per input? Not necessarily. Positive efficiency change only means that relative productivity has increased. One way to boost efficiency is indeed to improve productivity, but another comes with stalling leadership. If the industry leader slips in terms of productivity, the followers get closer and formally this shows as positive efficiency change! Think of deteriorating industry conditions. Examples abound. In the mining industry the quality of the ore lessens as time progresses, simply because the easiest available ores are mined first. Conditions may also deteriorate as a result of falling demand, particularly when a product approaches the end of its life cycle, with new substitutes taking over. And conditions are influenced by world markets. For example, if a low wage country enters the industry and the incumbents are sluggish in making adjustments, such as reallocations to newly developing economies, costs may press harder on smaller numbers of output.

Conversely, without any change in the firm, its efficiency may change. In fact, in a world of technical progress the best practice productivity increases, and since efficiency is productivity relative to the best practice, it will go down by the denominator effect if there is *no* change in the inputs or outputs of the firm we analyze. The Dutch proverb "Standstill is decline" is particularly relevant to the concept of efficiency, because the latter is a *relative* concept. When Henny Youngman was asked, "How is your wife?" and gave the answer, "Compared with what?" he was right if the question was meant to elicit an indication of her performance rather than some valuation against an absolute yardstick.

The underlying concept of productivity—output per unit of input—is an absolute concept, though. There are many physical examples. The fuel "efficiency" concept of miles per gallon is a productivity measure, indicating how much output we get per unit of input. If, however, the input and output are in the same dimension, as in energy conversion, we are back in the situation where the "best" is a ratio of one (1 Watt of converted energy per Watt of basic energy). Here a ratio equal to 1 represents the case of no waste, hence full efficiency. Another physical example of a productivity measure is tons harvested (say of rice) per acre. To assess whether it signals a good performance, we must know the size relative to the maximum observed magnitude, and *that* is efficiency.

Now let us bring in profitability, a third related concept. In the single input–single output duopoly, with firm 1 more productive than firm 2 ($y^1/x^1 > y^2/x^2$), is firm 1 necessarily more *profitable*? We must disentangle a number of issues.

First, there is the *size* issue. Firm 1 might enjoy a better margin between revenue and cost per unit of output (because it needs less input) and hence be the more profitable firm per unit of output, but firm 2 might have a bigger market share and hence generate a greater sum of profits. The size effect might outweigh the productivity effect. We correct for it by measuring profit per unit of sales. In other words, instead of profits $py - \underline{w}x$ we compare the profit *rates* $(py - \underline{w}x)/py$.

The second issue is the presence or absence of well-functioning markets, on both the input and the output side. If the firms face common market prices, on both the input and the output sides, we can compare the profit rate of the more productive firm, which is $(py^1 - \underline{w}x^1)/py^1$, with that of the less productive firm, namely $(py^2 - \underline{w}x^2)/py^2$, and conclude that the former is bigger. The proof of this inequality is easy: The leading terms are equal (namely 1), while the second terms are inverse productivities (x/y) with a common coefficient $(-\underline{w}/p)$. Inverse productivity is obviously negatively related to productivity, but the minus sign makes the relationship between productivity and profitability per unit sales a positive one.

However—and this takes us to the third issue—the relationship between efficiency and profitability breaks down the moment we drop the single input–single output assumption. Figure 4.1 (overleaf) provides a simple example.[1]

In Figure 4.1, three firms each produce one unit of output using two inputs, namely labor and capital. Firm 2 is inefficient, because it can contract its labor and capital inputs to the midpoint of techniques 1 and 3, as explained in Chapter 3. Then, by dividing its inputs between the techniques 1 and 3, it would produce ½ + ½ = 1 unit of output. However, if capital is very inexpensive relative to labor, firm 2 will be more profitable than firm 3, simply because it is more economical, using the inexpensive input, capital.

It makes a difference—even for multi input–multi output industries—if profits are based on accounting prices. It is

---

1   This is a simple variant on Figure 3.1, Chapter 3.

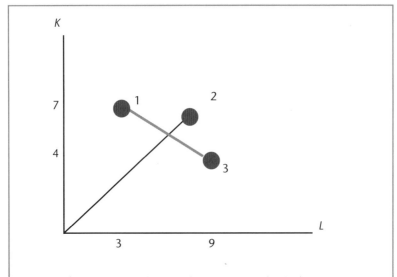

Figure 4.1 An industry with two inputs and a single output
Firms 1 and 3 are efficient. Firm 2 is not. Yet if labor is very expensive, input combination 3 is more costly than input combination 2.

commendable, because it restores the relationship between efficiency and profit per unit of sales. The key to the analysis is the result of Chapter 3, equation (17), which equates efficiency to the revenue/cost ratio at accounting prices. Simple manipulation modifies that equation into the following:

$$\frac{(p_1 y^1_1 + ... + p_l y^1_l) - (w_1 x^1_1 + ... + w_k x^1_k)}{(p_1 y^1_1 + ... + p_1 y^1_1)} = 1 - efficiency^{-1} \tag{18}$$

Because the right-hand side of equation (18) is positively related to efficiency (there are two minus signs!), we once more have a positive relationship between efficiency and profitability. But be careful. Under accounting prices, fully efficient decision making units break even and inefficient units operate at a loss. Indeed, if efficiency is 1 in formula (18), as is the case for fully efficient decision making units, then the right-hand side is 0, hence profit must be 0. If the efficiency is less than full, for example ¾, then the right hand side would be -$\frac{1}{3}$, creating a loss on the left-hand side.

It is not difficult to evaluate the expressions numerically, and I shall illustrate this for the example of Figure 4.1. Accounting prices can be computed using the zero profit conditions for the efficient decision making units. In Figure 4.1 the accounting profit of firm 1 is $1 - (3w + 7r)$, where w is the wage rate and r the rental rate, while the accounting profit of firm 3 is $1 - (9w + 4r)$.[2] Setting these two profits equal to zero, we obtain two simple equations: $3w + 7r = 1$ and $9w + 4r = 1$. The solution is $w = 1/17$ and $r = 2/17$. These figures can be used to calculate the total cost of firm 2, hence its accounting profit (which will be negative) and efficiency, using formula (18). Let us carry out the calculation. Reading Figure 4.1, firm 2's inputs are 7 units of labor and 6 of capital, hence its profit is $1 - (7/17 + 6 \times 2/17) = 1 - \textit{efficiency}^{-1}$, using formula (18). Solving, the efficiency of firm 2 amounts to 17/19. In general, the numbers are given simply as output by the linear programming routine.

The crucial difference between market prices and accounting prices is that the former are observed and the latter are not. Market prices are exogenous, meaning that they are considered given, as *data*. Accounting prices are endogenous, meaning that they are derived from the data: not from price data, but from input and output data. It is instructive to see the difference in the simple single input–single output duopoly, where firm 1's data are input x^1, output y^1, prices $\underline{w}^1$ and $\underline{p}^1$, and firm 2's data are x^2, y^2, $\underline{w}^2$ and $\underline{p}^2$. Different price normalizations are allowed. If we stick to Chapter 3, equation (14), it is $py^1 = 1$ and the zero profit condition, $py^1 - wx^1 = 0$, yields $w = py^1/x^1 = 1/x^1$.

Alternatively, the accounting prices $p = 1$ for the output and $w = y^1/x^1$ for the input may be employed, because it suffices that the relative prices remain the same. There are two ways to explain why this statement is true. One is via result (17) of Chapter 3, where efficiency was shown to be the revenue/cost *ratio*. This measure is clearly insensitive with respect to proportionate price changes. The other is to visualize a currency change. For example,

---

2   Revenue is 1 because of the single output variant of price normalization condition (14): see Chapter 3.

if firm 1 produces 100 kilograms of rice, then the normalization condition $py^1 = 1$ reads $p = 1/100 = 1$ cent per kilogram. Now we *could* choose this as a new currency unit; i.e. the cent instead of the dollar. Then the value of output would not be 1 but 100 cents and the price would be 1 cent or 0.01 only.

The bottom line is that accounting prices must be *derived* from quantity data, in a way such that the most productive firms break even. The upshot is that profitability tests of performance, or conversely profitability implications of performance, may be misleading when external, possibly distorted prices are used. This truth is apparent in the simple context of our single input–single output duopoly. If the less productive firm, firm 2, commands a lower input price, that is $\underline{w}^2 < \underline{w}^1$, it might be equally profitable or even more so than firm 1, if the input price discount is strong. The question arises what to do in such a situation. Is it advantageous to stimulate the *productive* firm 1, or the *profitable* firm 2? In other words, where should you put your money or allocate the resources?

The answer may vary with the setting, but we can make one general observation. *Both* firms would benefit from adopting the most productive technique. In the simple example this would not change a thing for firm 1 (which is already the best practice firm), but it clearly would make firm 2 more profitable. Firm 2 earns a profit of $\underline{p}^2 y^2 - \underline{w}^2 x^2$, but replacement of output y^2 by potential output $(y^1/x^1) \, x^2$ would add to the revenue term, hence increase profit. Here we recognize y^1/x^1 as the best-practice productivity. Alternatively, should the market not bear the additional output, the profit could be increased by cutting back input x^2 to what is necessary given the best practice technique, namely $(x^1/y^1) \, y^2$.[3] Here we recognize x^1/y^1 as the minimal technical coefficient.

The productivity and the technical coefficient are each other's inverse, which is no surprise, because productivity is basically output per unit of input and a technical coefficient is input required per unit of output. The lesson of this example is that to improve performance, we must be on the lookout for the most

---

3   The latter is indeed less than x^2 by assumption that firm 1 is more productive, $y^1/x^1 > y^2/x^2$.

productive practice, not the most profitable. This is the relevant rule of thumb even if the criterion is profit. In other words, the profit of a decision making unit is enhanced by adopting best practice techniques, not by adopting the most profitable practices. In our duopoly example the adoption of the technique of the most profitable firm (firm 2) would even be detrimental to the profit of firm 1!

This paradoxical relationship between productivity and profitability rests on the following fact: *we can copy techniques, but not prices.* Emerging economies rightly adopt western production practices in manufacturing and the service sectors, because like everyone they benefit from efficiency. Conversely, these western plants do not copy their eastern counterparts, even though they may be more profitable. The low wages prevailing in China and its southern neighbors cannot be copied. They are reflections of conditions beyond business control, such as the endowments of nations. If a nation is well endowed with labor relative to other resources such as minerals, local wages will be low. This argument is valid even in the absence of exploitation.

Within a single country, however, we can expect less variation in external conditions.

Case study 5: U.S. manufacturing

Foster, Haltiwanger and Syverson (2005) investigated the manufacturing of 11 products in the United States, selected on the basis of their homogeneity, namely corrugated and solid fiber boxes, white pan bread, carbon black, roasted coffee beans, ready-mixed concrete, oak flooring, motor gasoline, block ice, processed ice, hardwood plywood, and raw cane sugar.

They found a strong correlation between physical productivity and revenue/cost ratios. Revenue/cost ratios are positively correlated with product prices (not surprisingly), but physical productivity is negatively correlated with product prices. Basically, more efficient firms pass on their cost advantages to buyers. While new firms perform well in terms of profit (otherwise they would not make it), they score even better in terms of productivity.

The interplay between benchmarking-based efficiency analysis and statistics-based productivity analysis is subtle. Let me expand on this subject. Benchmarking is a linear programming technique that permits us to assess efficiency levels: that is, relative productivities. It is a deterministic procedure which accepts data at face value. Statistical analysis, however, explores relationships between variables, such as inputs, outputs, or prices, which are observed with measurement error, and therefore are modeled as random variables. It is possible to incorporate this statistical viewpoint into benchmarking. The theory of benchmarking in an environment of random data is called *stochastic frontier analysis*. As with basic benchmarking, the key ideas of stochastic frontier analysis can be explained by means of a simple example. I shall attempt no more than to convey these key ideas. Stochastic frontier analysis is a developed branch of econometrics, with numerous sub-branches, but here I can only mention it and refer interested readers to further literature.

Let us return to a single input–single output organization, where decision making units i (where $i = 1, ..., I$) have labor inputs x_i and outputs $y_i = \beta x_i - u_i$. Let coefficient β represent the best practice output–input ratio, the productivity of the most efficient unit. Then the quantity βx_i represents the potential output of unit i. Actual output may be less, and this is reflected in the subtraction of an amount u_i from potential output. In other words, the term u_i represents the non-realized output potential or inefficiency. It is assumed to be nonnegative.

Aigner and Chu (1968) were the first to propose an estimation procedure. Their idea is that productivity parameter β is selected so as to get the closest fit in the sense of minimizing the sum of the discrepancies. They minimize $(\beta x_1 - y_1) + ... + (\beta x_I - y_I)$ subject to the constraints $\beta x_1 - y_1, ..., \beta x_I - y_I \geq 0$. The sum of discrepancies is minimized by the lowest admissible value of β. The constraints are fulfilled if and only if $\beta x_1 \geq y_1, ..., \beta x_I \geq y_I$, which in turn is true if and only if $\beta \geq y_1/x_1, ..., \beta \geq y_I/x_I$. The lowest β for which this string of inequalities holds is max $(y_1/x_1, ..., y_I/x_I)$. This value is used to estimate β. It is simply the best practice productivity. For multiple inputs several production parameters have to be estimated simultaneously, and the solution to the linear program requires a tool; Excel's Solver, discussed in Chapter 2, serves this purpose.

Although they employ an econometric model, Aigner and Chu (1968) basically follow the benchmarking technique of using the best practices to estimate the production parameters and to estimate the inefficiency of the other units. The implicit assumption is that observed best practices are efficient. It is possible, however, that in an organization all decision making units suffer from some degree of inefficiency. If you think about it, it is quite a big assumption to identify the best conceivable practice with the best observed practice. One absurd implication of this implicit assumption is that a monopolist would always be efficient, because as the only one in town it is automatically the best observed practice! To permit inefficiencies, econometricians have added another term to the equation, which thus becomes $y_i = \beta x_i - u_i + v_i$. Output equals the sum of potential output, an inefficiency term, plus an error term. This model separates sources of inefficiencies and of errors of measurement, which seems a natural idea.

In this approach it is assumed that the inputs are measured precisely, which is not a bad assumption for the most important input, labor services, but that the output is not measured precisely, but with an error of measurement given by the term v_i. This assumption is reminiscent of regression analysis, but there are some important subtleties that distinguish it. For one, it may well be that the productivity parameter continues to be estimated best by the best practice productivity—unit i with the greatest value of y_i/x_i—but this does not preclude the possibility that the best practice is inefficient. For this unit we would have $y_i = \beta x_i$, but in the present context this only means that the sum of the inefficiency term and the error of measurement term is 0! Unit i seems to produce the maximum possible output (given its input), but further statistical analysis may lead us to conclude that output has been overreported. After correction for the estimated error of measurement, the true output is seen to be smaller than the reported output, the unit is no longer declared to be fully efficient and there is scope for state-of-the-art technology application.

Unlike the inefficiency term, the error term can go either way. There can overreporting or underreporting. Standard practice is to assume that the error term is drawn from the well-known bell shaped normal distribution. Stochastic frontier analysts assume that the inefficiency term of a decision making unit (u_i) can also be modeled as a drawing from a distribution. However, since the inefficiency term is nonnegative it cannot be taken from the two-sided normal distribution, and it is customary to assume that the inefficiency term is drawn from a truncated distribution, the half-normal. The procedure is pragmatic, and does not have any theoretical foundation. It may be wrong, and therefore stochastic frontier analysis suffers from the problem of specification error.

The different shapes of the two distributions—normal and half-normal—facilitate estimation of their parameters. To grasp this, first assume, on the contrary, that both distributions are normal. Now it is a well-known fact that a linear combination of normally distributed variables is normally distributed as well. Hence regression analysis can be applied to estimate the mean and variance of the combination of the inefficiency term and the error-of-measurement term, but there would be no way to identify the separate terms. When we impose the condition that the inefficiency term only makes negative contributions, the distribution of the sum of the terms gets twisted to the left. This skews the overall distribution, and the degree of skewness is determined by the relative importance of the inefficiency component. For this reason measurement of the skewness enables estimation of the two parameters of the inefficiency distribution. More precisely, Aigner, Lovell, and Schmidt (1977) show that the ratio of the standard deviation parameter of the truncated normal distribution of the efficiency term to the standard deviation parameter of the normal distribution—a measure of the skewness—is featured by the likelihood function. Since the sum of the variances also enters the likelihood function, it is possible to disentangle the two effects (by estimating both the ratio and the sum).

Initially it was thought that the skewness effect would be too weak to make sound statistical inferences, but the results are surprisingly sharp, at least for organizations with many units, such as banks or hotel chains. Stochastic formulas can replace the simple DEA-based expressions of this book, but it would complicate the analysis, and therefore I refer interested readers to Kumbhakar and Lovell's (2003) text.

Even though it is possible to combine benchmarking with stochastic analysis, and it is done, simple DEA remains surprisingly resilient. There are a number of reasons. A great advantage of DEA-based benchmarking is that for every decision making unit the best practices can be identified. This is a great source for learning. Detailed comparison with the benchmarks is possible, and it highlights the slacks, such as quantities of inputs that can be saved. A second advantage of simple DEA is its simplicity. You can benchmark after reading this simple, slim book, whereas stochastic frontier analysis requires familiarity with econometrics and not just the basics, but quite some advanced material. A third, related reason is that DEA-based benchmarking requires no specification of the functional form for the production function. For this reason DEA is called a non-parametric method. The above discussion's single input assumption circumvented the need to aggregate inputs by means of a production function, but in general stochastic frontier analysis demands some hard choices, and this brings in further specification errors. Last but not least, there is a pragmatic reason for the persistent popularity of DEA, namely that although stochastic frontier analysis may be theoretically superior, it does not necessarily produce different results.

Case study 6: U.S. hotels

Anderson and his colleagues (1999) analyzed a varied sample of 48 hotels in the United States. A single output (total revenue) was produced with six inputs, namely the number of full-time equivalent employees, the number of rooms, total gaming-related expenses, total food and beverage expenses, and other expenses. Using the technique of stochastic frontier analysis, they found an average efficiency score of 89 percent.

This result coincides precisely with the result of the only hotel efficiency study that they knew of, Morey and Dittman's (1995) DEA study of 54 hotels of a United States chain from a geographically dispersed area. It may have been luck, with different factors offsetting each other; even the data sets are different.

Case study 7: European railway efficiency

A cleaner comparison of DEA and stochastic frontier analysis is seen in a study by Coelli and Perelman (1999). They applied the two techniques of DEA and stochastic frontier analysis to a common data set, namely that of the European railways. Their data series involved annual data on 17 companies observed over the six-year period from 1988 to 1993. Two outputs were considered, passenger services and freight services, and three inputs: labor, equipment, and capital. In their own words, they "do not observe a lot of differences in the technical efficiencies obtained using the various methods."

Coelli and Perelman (1999, p. 335) proposed to take geometric means of the various results, an idea borrowed from the time-series forecasting literature (where many authors contend that the average of the predictions from a number of models will often outperform any one particular predictive model). Thus they found a mean technical efficiency level of 82 percent, with mean values for individual companies ranging from 61 percent for Greece to 94 percent for Switzerland.

The figures in case study 7 assumed constant returns to scale, in line with the theory of this chapter. Chapter 6 will discuss alternative assumptions.

Further reading

The literature started with an analysis of production frontiers: see Färe, Grosskopf and Lovell (1994) and antecedents given there. A comprehensive text covering the material discussed in this chapter is Coelli *et al.* (2005). It covers stochastic frontier analysis. As mentioned, a good specialized text on the latter subject is Kumbhakar and Lovell (2003). There is also an interesting, but quite advanced, statistical approach to DEA directly, in Simar and Wilson (2000) and their further work. I recommend Ray (2004) again for a simple exposition.

5

RANKING

Ranking is a persuasive management tool which provides a sense of direction and infiltrates all corners of the information society. This chapter discusses the subtleties that surround this major application of benchmarking. The basic idea is simple, to calculate the efficiencies of decision making units and to line them up between 0 to 100 percent, but there is a nasty complication. Efficiency is measured by the revenue/cost ratio at accounting prices—see Chapter 3, equation (17)—but these prices vary across decision making units.

Central management has good reasons to use uniform prices, which apply indiscriminately to all business units. Since accounting prices give weight to alternative scores, it is natural for each decision making unit to want high weight to be given to performance components it is good at. It is not easy to find a compromise—although this chapter will show a way out—but it is harder, if not pointless, to accept differently scored weights for the different decision making units we are presuming to compare. That is the first reason.

Second, uniform prices will signal value to the entire organization rather than just to individual decision making units. This aspect is closely related to the issue of rent seeking. Certain types of personnel may claim their services are very valuable to the performance of the decision making unit where they are employed, because they are irreplaceable. They may even back up their claim by creating artificial scarcities. Certifications, licenses and closed shops are examples of this practice. Often quality considerations are invoked to justify them, but for right or for wrong, they create artificial constraints. Artificial or not, constraints carry a shadow price. The uniform valuations proposed in this chapter neutralize this type of distortion.

For the development of our theory it is useful to recollect why accounting prices are specific to decision making units. We have seen that benchmarking involves a linear program that determines the maximal expansion of a decision making unit, attainable by the adoption of best practices. The accounting prices fulfill equation (13) of Chapter 3, which was a straightforward application of the dual equation of linear programming, (11) of Chapter 2. And there accounting prices were seen to be marginal productivities.[1] In particular, the accounting price of an input measures how much more output could be produced if an extra unit of the input were available. Now if an input is scarce in a decision making unit, it acts as a bottleneck, and therefore carries a high accounting price. Since the mix of inputs may differ across decision making units, an input may be relatively scarce somewhere and abundant elsewhere. This is why accounting price varies across units.

This perhaps rather abstract discussion can be made very concrete by means of the example we used for Figure 3.1 in Chapter 3, which is reproduced here as Figure 5.1, with a little detail added.

By assumption, all the units in Figure 5.1 produce one unit of output. Decision making unit 2 can produce its output using only 80% of its inputs by using the techniques of decision making units 1 and 3, while decision making unit 4 would need

---

1   See the main theorem of linear programming, equation (8) (page 21) and the ensuing discussion.

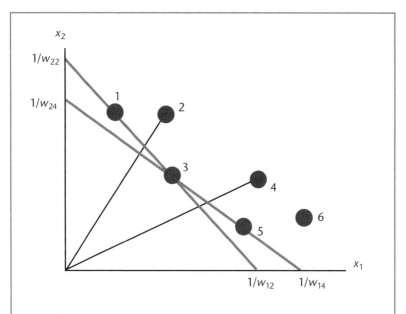

Figure 5.1 An organization with two inputs and a single output
Decision making units 1, 3, and 5 use little input. Decision making units 2, 4, and 6 are inefficient.

only some 75% of its inputs if it employed the techniques of decision making units 3 and 5. The point is that the benchmarks are different—units 1 and 3 in the first case, and units 3 and 5 in the second. Now in Chapter 4 we saw how accounting prices can be derived from the condition that they enable benchmarks to break even (and render inefficient units unprofitable). From this requirement we can conclude that unit 2's accounting prices are different from those of unit 4. The precise reasoning is as follows.

We can see from price normalization equation (14) of Chapter 3 that the value of the inputs of the benchmarks for unit 2, which are given by points 1 and 3 in Figure 5.1, must be 1. It follows that all points on the line segment connecting points 1 and 3 have the value 1 as well. Now the horizontal and vertical intercepts of this \$1 line are $1/w_{12}$ and $1/w_{22}$, respectively, where

w_{12} and w_{22} represent the prices of inputs 1 and 2 when unit 2 is benchmarked. *Here the first subscript indexes the item that is priced and the second subscript indexes the decision making unit.* If we benchmark the next most inefficient decision making unit, unit 4, the accounting prices that make the relevant best practices break even (those of decision making units 3 and 5) are determined by the straight line through points 3 and 5.

From the intercepts in Figure 5.1 we see that $w_{12} > w_{14}$ and $w_{22} < w_{24}$. In other words, decision making unit 2 has a relatively high accounting price for input 1, and decision making unit 4 has a relatively high accounting price for input 2. The reason is that input 1 is scarce in unit 2 while input 2 is scarce in unit 4, as can be seen from the slopes of the straight lines connecting points 2 and 4 with the origin. When an input is scarce, it helps a lot to have an additional unit. Its marginal productivity is great.[2] Since marginal productivities and accounting prices are equal, this explains why these prices vary across decision making units. The accounting prices of a decision making unit are idiosyncratic.

The spread in input accounting prices is very useful information for the central management of a company with different business units. One of the tasks of central management is to reallocate resources from less to more efficient units. Less efficient units underperform. They could produce more given their inputs. Another point of view is that they need less input given their outputs and that the excess resources can be transferred out. The performance of the company is best served by reallocating them to the most efficient units. Since several units may be equally efficient candidate recipients, central management faces the question which unit gets which resource. Here the accounting prices can be used as a tool. The rule of thumb is as follows.

> Reallocate the excess resources of less efficient business units to an efficient unit where the accounting price is relatively high.

The rationale of this rule of thumb is that resources are best put to

---

2   See Chapter 2, formula (8) and the ensuing discussion.

work where they are most productive and *accounting* prices are equal to marginal productivities. Market prices do not have the power to signal where resources are best put to work, simply because they are equal for the different business units.

While the reallocation of resources makes perfect sense from the viewpoint of production process performance optimization, it also provides the right incentives. Most managers appreciate extended control over company resources. If benchmarking is an integrated management tool, this mechanism yields an incentive to run business units efficiently, on top of financial bonus plans. The two can be combined. Benchmarking can be used not only to weed out production and organization inefficiencies, but also to design bonus plans, as we have seen in the case of Spanish restaurants (Chapter 3, page 36).

The idiosyncrasy of accounting prices is often overlooked, but it is a serious problem. In the absence of uniform prices, it is not clear how we must *rank* the units. For illustration, consider decision making units 2 and 4 in Figure 5.1. Their efficiency levels are 80% and 75% respectively, but these figures are based on different weights for the inputs. A similar problem plagues the output side, at least when there are multiple outputs. Figure 3.2 from Chapter 3, reproduced overleaf as Figure 5.2 (with detail added), makes the point.

By assumption, all units use one unit of input. In Figure 5.2, decision making unit 1 is slightly more efficient than decision making unit 5 (which could expand its output quite a bit using a mixture of the practices 3 and 4). But look at the accounting prices: $p_{11} < p_{15}$ while $p_{21} > p_{25}$. Decision making unit 1 has a higher accounting price for product 2 and decision making unit 5's is higher for product 1. The story is similar on the input side, but the orderings are opposite.

In Chapter 3 we calculated the ratios of accounting prices in Figures 3.2 and 5.2. The straight line through points 2 and 3 implied that for this pair of benchmarks, output 2 is relatively expensive, namely $p_{21}/p_{11} = 1.33$.[3] Similarly, decision making unit 5

---

3   In fact, since the output coordinates of decision making units are precisely the data of the managers' outputs in Chapter 2 which we analyzed using Excel, the precise accounting prices were seen to be $p_{11} = 0.016$ and $p_{21} = 0.021$ (see Chapter 2, Figure 2.5).

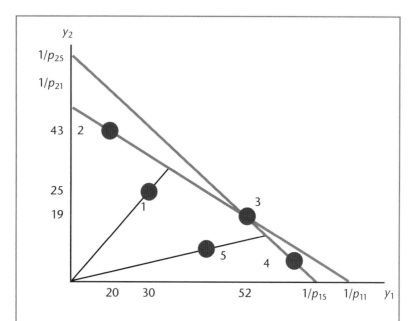

Figure 5.2 An organization with a single input and two outputs
Decision making units 2, 3, and 4 produce much output. Decision making
units 1 and 5 are inefficient.

has accounting prices which were determined by the steeper straight line through points 3 and 4 (with slope -45°), which translated into a lower relative accounting price for output 2 (in fact $p_{21}/p_{11} = 1$), hence the higher relative accounting price for output 1. Since decision making unit 5 is the one generating more of output 1, we may conclude that:

Idiosyncratic accounting prices are higher for outputs which are produced relatively abundantly.

This result is perhaps paradoxical, because we tend to associate abundance with low prices. The negative relationship between quantity and price is a property of demand functions, whereas here we are analyzing the supply side of a firm. Then the relationship is opposite. In Chapter 2, particularly towards the end, we learned that accounting prices of outputs reflect the costs of producing them. Now if a decision making unit produces a lot of a certain type of output, it lays claim on the resources that are used intensively in their production. These resources will be scarce if we analyze the decision making unit by itself. Scarcity means a high resource price, and this translates into a high idiosyncratic accounting price.

This result can be used to provide a foundation to the tendency we noted earlier, of decision making units giving more weight to score dimensions in which they perform relatively well. In fact, the classic Ratio DEA model formalizes the concept of self-preferred weighting (Charnes, Cooper, and Rhodes, 1978). This model defines the efficiency of decision making unit i—with input vector x^i and output vector y^i—as the revenue–cost ratio uy^i/vx^i, where the weights of the outputs (listed in row vectors u) and the weights of the inputs (listed in row vectors v) are selected to maximize the ratio, subject to the constraints that the ratios uy^j/vx^j are less than 1 for all decision making units j. The weights are selected to get the best score. The approach taken here is to let the weights be determined by the underlying primal program that calculates the potential output level of the decision making units. This way they have a nice economic interpretation, namely as marginal productivity. Both approaches produce idiosyncratic weights, but for the accounting prices approach there is a simple way to iron out the differences.[4]

Let us recall the formal framework. We have decision making units i with input vectors x^i and output vectors y^i. We calculate the maximally producible output ey^i, given the input x^i and the practices (x^i, y^i): see program (12) of Chapter 3. Here the symbol e stands for the expansion factor to be maximized. The dual

---

4   Charnes et al. (1978) show that the two approaches are essentially dual to each other. In their aptly entitled paper "The law of one price in data envelopment analysis," Kuosmanen, Cherchye, and Sipiläinen (2006) equalize accounting prices between decision making units by first taking a dual version of the efficiency linear program and then imposing price equalities. My approach is simpler.

equation—(13) of Chapter 3—generates the accounting prices of the inputs, $w_1, ..., w_k$, and of the outputs, $p_1, ..., p_l$. (Here k and l are the numbers of the inputs and the outputs, respectively.) The problem is that these prices are specific to the object we benchmark— decision making unit I—because inputs may be scarce at some decision making units and abundant at others, and outputs may be produced in costly volumes.

Formally, the decision making unit constraints of program (12) read

$$x^1_1\theta_1 +...+ x^I_1\theta_I \le x^1_1, ..., x^1_k\theta_1 +...+ x^I_k\theta_I \le x^1_k, \tag{19}$$
$$y^1_1\theta_1 +...+ y^I_1\theta_I \ge y^1_1e, ..., y^1_l\theta_1+...+ y^I_l\theta_I \ge y^1_le.$$

In inequalities (19) the symbols $\theta_1, ..., \theta_I$ are the variables in the thought experiment where we run the decision making units with intensities $\theta_1, ..., \theta_I$ subject to the inputs available to the decision making unit we benchmark, unit 1 in this case, and the requirement that the components of (expanded) output vector ey^1 are produced. The right-hand sides of inequalities (19) are specific to the decision making unit, and prompt the accounting prices to be idiosyncratic.

There is a way out, as follows. Imagine that we have the power to improve the performance of decision making units not only by letting them adopt best practices, but also by reallocating resources between them. A bank consists of branches, and we not only force each branch to be efficient, we can also free its resources by closing it or at least trimming it down. The formal analysis involves the assessment of the overall efficiency of the bank by calculating how much more total output it could produce given the total input. Instead of benchmarking a branch on its peers, we benchmark the entire bank. The benchmarking continues to be done on the same reference group of peers: that is, on its own branches and *not* on other banks. This procedure amounts to replacement of the right-hand sides of constraints (19) by the *total* organization resources or inputs $x_1, ..., x_k$ and (potential) outputs $ey_1, ..., ey_k$, where e is the expansion factor, as before. These total figures are defined by the following equations:

$$x_1 = x^1_1 + \ldots + x^l_1, \ldots, x_k = x^1_k + \ldots + x^l_k, \tag{20}$$
$$y_1 = y^1_1 + \ldots + y^l_1, \ldots, y_k = y^1_l + \ldots + y^l_l.$$

The overall efficiency of the organization is the inverse of the expansion factor, e, where the latter is the solution to benchmarking program (12) with equation (20) used to modify the right-hand sides:

$$\max_{\theta_1, \ldots, \theta_l, e \geq 0} e: \tag{21}$$
$$x^1_1 \theta_1 + \ldots + x^l_1 \theta_l \leq x_1, \ldots, x^1_k \theta_1 + \ldots + x^l_k \theta_l \leq x_k$$
$$y^1_1 \theta_1 + \ldots + y^l_1 \theta_l \geq y_1 e, \ldots, y^1_l \theta_1 + \ldots + y^l_l \theta_l \geq y_l e$$

As we did in Chapter 3 for decision making unit 1, we can associate input and output accounting prices $w_1, \ldots, w_k$ and $p_1, \ldots, p_l$ with benchmarking program (21). The attractive property of these prices is that they measure the marginal productivity of inputs and outputs to the organization as a whole. The accounting prices constructed in this way are independent of the decision making unit under consideration.

The resolution of the weighting problem rests on the replacement of decision making units' scarcities and abundances by their overall counterparts. Let me explain the procedure for the organization with two inputs and a single output displayed in Figure 5.1. The first three decision making units, 1, 2, and 3, are well endowed with the second input, and the last three, 4, 5, and 6, with the first. The points in Figure 5.1 represent the available quantities of the two inputs.[5]

The coordinates of these decision making unit points are the following.[6] For unit 1: (1, 3); for unit 2: (2, 3); for unit 3: (2, 2); for unit 4: (4, 2); for unit 5: (4, 1); and for unit 6 (5, 1). Summing the first components we see that the total endowment of input 1 amounts to 18 and of input 2 to 12. There are three benchmarks, namely units 1, 3, and 5. The first two are relevant to unit 2, since unit 2 could contract its inputs by employing the practices

---

5   I maintain the assumption that all units produce a single unit of output.
6   The rounding does not affect the result.

of 1 and 3, and the latter two are the benchmarks for units 4 (and 6), as was analyzed in Chapter 3 (Figure 3.1, reproduced with added detail as Figure 5.1). The endowment intensity of unit 2 (2 units of input 1 to 3 units of input 2) is in between the intensities of its benchmarks, units 1 and 3, and the endowment intensity of unit 4 (4 to 2) is in between the intensities of its benchmarks, units 3 and 5. The overall endowment intensity (18 to 12) is also between the intensities of benchmarks 3 and 5. It follows that the zero-profit conditions of the latter two benchmarks determine the accounting prices of the organization. They coincide with the accounting prices of decision making unit 4. The proportion of its endowment is not too far from the overall endowment proportion.

For a single-output organization, the accounting prices of a decision making unit with a representative mix of inputs are the ones that reflect the values to the organization as a whole, in the sense of marginal productivities. An analogous observation can be made for a single input–multiple output organization. *The performance weights generated by the benchmarking program of a decision making unit with a representative mix of scores agree with the optimal ones (relevant to the organization as a whole).* There is no need to identify the decision making unit of which the accounting prices can be used in order to measure and compare the performance of all units. It suffices to solve the organization's benchmarking program, (21). The output contains the shadow prices.

Having settled the issue of weighting performance dimensions, let us now tackle the issue of ranking. We employ the input and output accounting prices $w_1, ..., w_k$ and $p_1, ..., p_l$ associated with benchmarking program (21). The efficiency of decision making unit 1 is given by the revenue/cost ratio (17) of Chapter 3, reproduced here for convenience:

$$efficiency = (p_1 y^1_1 + ... + p_l y^1_l) / (w_1 x^1_1 + ... + w_k x^1_k)^- \qquad (22)$$

In formula (22) the weights are truly independent of the decision making unit! The decision making units are considered as machines which transform inputs into outputs. The outputs are aggregated using the weights p_1, ..., p_l and the inputs with the weights w_1, ..., w_k. Expression (22) measures efficiency as aggregated output per unit of aggregated input. The theory of Chapter 4 applies, in particular the observation that efficiency is a measure between 0 and 1. The reason is that the duality analysis—see equation (15) of Chapter 3—by which the value of the outputs is less than or equal to the value of the inputs, happens to be *independent* of the object that is benchmarked (that is, decision making unit 1 in Chapter 3 or the entire organization in the present chapter).

The final step is to rank the decision units from 0 to 1 on the basis of formula (22). The amazing achievement of our analysis is that the performance measure weights used in the ranking are not only common to all the decision making units we rank, but are determined by the analysis. For example, university departments quarrel about the weights education and research should get in ranking their performances. Business schools quarrel about the weights starting salaries of their graduates fetch relative to other scores, such as faculty citations. The Balanced Scorecard of Kaplan and Norton (2005) measures business performance in four dimensions: not only financial, but also customer satisfaction, internal business processes (for instance, measured by speed), and learning and growth (measured by, for example, employees' morale), and it is not clear how to weigh the different scores. Although this decomposition is to some degree a strategic management tool, there may be instances where trade-offs between different performance scores must be weighed. In such cases we do not want to peg the relative importance of the different dimensions, and our benchmarking approach can be invoked to determine the weights.

Case study 8: Dutch economics and business schools

A fine illustration of ranking analysis is a recent paper by Kuosmanen, Cherchye, and Sipiläinen (2006), who examined the productive efficiency of research in economics and business management faculties of Dutch universities. They evaluated the efficiency of 79 research programs organized at eight universities, and took the revenue-share weighted average of the programs per university. The inputs were (1) junior research staff (PhD candidates) and (2) senior research staff (other research personnel). The outputs were (1) total number of doctoral dissertations, (2) total number of refereed articles in top international journals, and (3) total number of refereed articles in other international journals. They modified the basic model slightly to accommodate increasing returns to scale. (We shall deal with such a modification in the next chapter ,and see that it affects the format of the value equations little.) In their first table Kuosmanen and colleagues show that the relative accounting prices of junior and senior staff are 40% and 60%, respectively.

As for all accounting prices, these percentages reflect the relative productivities, not necessarily the actual wages. In this case, however, the authors suggest that the rewards follow productivity quite closely, noting that:

> These shadow prices are well in line with the official salary tables stated in the collective labor agreement. Indeed, the starting salaries of the junior staff are approximately two thirds of the starting salaries of the senior staff in all salary categories.

Table 5.1 gives the ranks of the different universities by efficiency of economics and business management research:

It is also possible to group the research programs not by university, but by field. This produces Table 5.2.

These rankings are based on input and output measurements and benchmarking calculations. Valuations are generated as shadow prices of the benchmarking program, and indeed have been reported for the inputs, junior and senior staff.

Table 5.1 Efficiency differences across universities

University	No. of observations	Efficiency
Tilburg University	27	0.806
Wageningen University	21	0.616
Free University of Amsterdam	36	0.596
University of Groningen	18	0.560
Erasmus University Rotterdam	59	0.552
University of Maastricht	27	0.478
University of Nijmegen	6	0.465
University of Amsterdam	41	0.365

Source: Kuosmanen, Cherchye, and Sipiläinen (2006).

Table 5.2 Efficiency differences across fields of specialization

Field	No. of observations	Efficiency
Theoretical and Applied Microeconomics	21	0.832
Econometrics	15	0.810
Spatial and Environmental Economics	18	0.689
Macroeconomics, Money and International Issues	18	0.659
Development, Growth and Transition	15	0.590
Applied Mathematics	18	0.536
Marketing and Business Economics	66	0.534
Accounting and Finance	36	0.500
Applied Labor Economics	13	0.388
Economics of Public Policy	9	0.324

Source: Kuosmanen, Cherchye and Sipiläinen (2006).

Further reading

For further reading I suggest the Adler, Friedman, and Sinuany-Stern (2002) review of ranking methods in the DEA context. It is a bit mechanical. The use of accounting prices to weigh alternative scores proposed in this chapter simplifies ranking procedures. It is original to the best of my knowledge.

6

RETURNS TO SCALE

We have now removed the ambiguity that surrounds the concept of benchmarking and interrelated it with other concepts, including productivity, efficiency, and profitability. Basically we calculated for a decision making unit how much more it could yield if it adopted the best available practices. The difference between this so-called potential output and the recorded output has been the basis for measuring the underutilized capacity of the unit, or its inefficiency. The accounting prices generated by the linear program were used to express the efficiency of the decision making unit as a revenue/cost ratio, and when the entire organization is benchmarked, as a ranking device. The simplicity of the analysis was a result of the assumption of constant returns to scale. In this chapter we relax that assumption.

There are four types of returns to scale: constant returns, decreasing returns, increasing returns, and variable returns. The principles are understood most easily for a single input–single output production unit, like an old fashioned, non-automated delivery service, where the input is labor, denoted by x, and the output is parcel deliveries, denoted by y. I first discuss constant, decreasing, and increasing returns, keeping the important case of variable returns for later analysis.

In Figure 6.1, graph (a) represents the case of *constant returns to scale*. An increase in the input quantity yields a proportionate increase in the output quantity. Graph (b) represents the case of *decreasing returns to scale*. Here the returns of additional input are less than proportionate: for example 1% of extra input yields only 0.9% of extra output. Graph (c) represents the case of *increasing returns to scale*, where the returns become more than proportionate.

Since productivity is measured by output per unit of input, it is determined by the slope of the curve that connects a point of the graph with the origin. In graph (a) these curves all coincide with the straight line that represents the production function. In graph (b) the curve turns flatter as more input is employed: productivity decreases. In graph (c) the curve turns steeper, and therefore productivity increases. In(c) we speak of scale economies, whereas in (b) there are scale diseconomies.

The technique of benchmarking, in its narrow sense of data envelopment analysis (DEA), has a relationship with the issue of returns to scale. The relationship has two facets, which are posi-

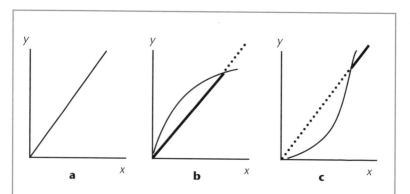

Figure 6.1 Constant, decreasing, and increasing returns to scale defined

In each panel input is along the horizontal axis and output along the vertical. The unbroken lines are below the production function. The thin dashed lines are above the production function, and therefore not feasible.

tioned under a slight angle and yield a spectrum of insights. In the first facet of the relationship the returns to scale are taken as the point of departure; it is assumed that the situation reflects one of the graphs in Figure 6.1.

If there are constant returns to scale—as in (a)—any feasible activity, represented by an input–output combination (x, y) on the graph (or under it, but that would be wasteful) can be run with *any* nonnegative intensity, θ. If (x, y) is feasible, then so are $(\theta x, \theta y)$ with $\theta = 0$.[1] In other words, if a point is feasible, then so is any other point on the *half-line* through that point and the origin. However, if there are decreasing returns to scale—as in (b)—any feasible activity can only be run with *lower* intensity. In other words, if (x, y) is feasible, then so are $(\theta x, \theta y)$ with $0 \le \theta \le 1$. If a point is feasible, then so is any other point on the unbroken line *segment* connecting that point with the origin. Finally, if there are increasing returns to scale—as in (c)—any feasible activity can only be run with *higher* intensity. If (x, y) is feasible, then so are $(\theta x, \theta y)$ with $\theta \ge 1$. In other words, if a point is feasible, then so is any other point on the unbroken *outer half-line* through the point, away from the origin. These observations are summarized in Table 6.1.

Table 6.1 Returns to scale and feasible intensities

Returns to scale	Feasible intensities	Geometry	Graph in Figure 6.1
Constant	$\theta \ge 0$	Half-line	(a)
Decreasing	$0 \le \theta \le 1$	Line segment	(b)
Increasing	$\theta \ge 1$	Outer half-line	(c)

The second facet of the relationship between scale economies (or diseconomies) takes *data* as the point of departure. We can organize the observations of input and output combinations in a

---

1    $(\theta x, \theta y)$ can be denoted briefly by $\theta(x, y)$.

scatter diagram. Figure 6.2 provides three examples, representing different industries.

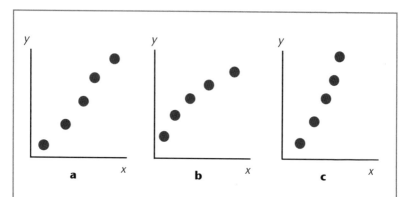

Figure 6.2 Constant, decreasing, and increasing returns to scale observed In each panel input is along the horizontal axis and output along the vertical

Visual inspection of Figure 6.2 suggests that the industries feature constant, decreasing, and increasing return to scale respectively. If we were to fit curves econometrically, these hypotheses would indeed be confirmed. Nevertheless, it is possible that in any of the three diagrams we might have any of the three types of return to scale! This would yield 3×3 = 9 possible graphs. Let me show just the three graphs that can come with one of the diagrams, say (c) in Figure 6.2.

Figure 6.3 replicates the *same* data points as in (c) of Figure 6.2. Graph (d) assumes constant returns to scale. Since the northeastern observation has the greatest productivity (output per input, y/x), the set of feasible points is bounded above by the half-line through this observation, as indicated. The first four data points represent inefficient observations, under the assumption of constant returns to scale. If we assume decreasing returns to scale, Table 6.1 tells us that we have only the line segments between the observed points and the origin in mapping the set of feasible points. This yields graph (e) of Figure 6.3. The only effect of assuming decreasing returns to scale instead of constant returns is

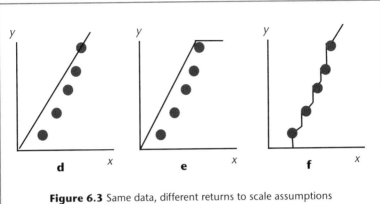

Figure 6.3 Same data, different returns to scale assumptions
In (d) constant returns are assumed, in (e) decreasing returns, and in (f)
increasing returns

that the production function is truncated, but that is due to the special nature of the data set (featuring ever more productive units). Perhaps more natural is the imposition of increasing returns to scale. Table 6.1 tells us that we have to insert the outer half-lines in the data points, away from the origin. In (f) these five half-lines have been inserted. Since they are all oriented such that the imaginary extension in a southwesterly direction hits the origin, the half-lines are steeper for the data points representing more productive observations, the ones further out in Figure 6.3. When we reach the input level of the next observation, the output jumps to the quantity produced by that observation, as indicated by the little vertical line segments.

Not surprisingly, the assumption of increasing returns to scale (defined in (c) in Figure 6.1) gives the closest fit to the scatter diagram, as (f) in Figure 6.3 shows. Similarly, if we were to analyze (b) in Figure 6.2, we would find that the assumption of decreasing returns gives the closest fit.

Now let me turn to the case of variable returns. First I review some basic production theory. A flexible form for a production function is the S-shaped function. It features first increasing and eventually decreasing returns to scale: see Figure 6.4.

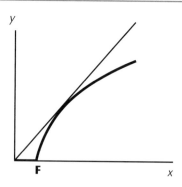

Figure 6.4 An S-shaped production function
Input is along the horizontal axis and output along the vertical. There is a fixed cost (F).

In Figure 6.4 a minimum quantity of input, F, is required to produce any positive amount of output, however little. This is called the *fixed cost* or *overhead*. Now, if output is increased, the fixed cost can be spread among more units and this causes the returns to scale initially to increase. The effect peters out, though. For big corporations overhead costs—however sizable in an absolute sense—become a small percentage of total cost, and another scale effect sets in: bottlenecks. Some inputs are just very hard to increase—think of land—and eventually they limit output as the variable inputs are increased. At some intermediate level the two scale effects balance, and productivity (output–input ratio y/x) is maximal. This is where the line to the origin is steepest: see the straight line in Figure 6.4. To the left of this point of tangency the returns to scale are increasing, and to the right they are decreasing. It may be that there is a *region* where productivity is maximal, as in Figure 6.5.

With a little imagination we can recognize an S-shape in Figures 6.4 and 6.5. Better known is the so-called U-shaped average cost curve, but it is just the other side of the coin. The reason is simple: Average cost is determined by input per unit of output, which is x/y or inverse productivity. Since productivity is

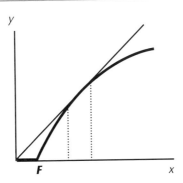

Figure 6.5 Another S-shaped production function

Input is along the horizontal axis and output along the vertical. In the region between the dashed lines productivity is maximal.

initially increasing and eventually decreasing, average cost is also initially decreasing and eventually increasing, so the curve made by plotting it is U-shaped. The U-shaped average cost curve associated with the production function in Figure 6.5 has a flat bottom.

The S-shaped production function is realistic, because it combines set-up costs with bottleneck effects. It is also flexible, because the point of maximal productivity might be reached when input is arbitrarily small—in which case the returns to scale are decreasing right away—or when input is arbitrarily large—in which case the returns to scale remain increasing for all relevant levels of activity. In other words, the S-shaped production function *encompasses* the cases of both decreasing and increasing returns. In this sense it is quite general, and it is desirable to have a counterpart in a multi input–multi output framework for efficiency measurement.

The counterpart exists, and is called *variable returns to scale*. The model is due to Afriat (1972) and Førsund and Hjalmarsson (1974), and has been launched in a DEA setting by Färe, Grosskopf, and Logan (1983) and Banker, Charnes, and Cooper (1984). The idea is that fixed costs cannot be dissolved by running decision making units, including their inputs, at small intensities. We can combine decision making units, but the level of operation must remain the same. Formally, the sum of the intensities must be 1. A simple example should make this clearer: see Figure 6.6.

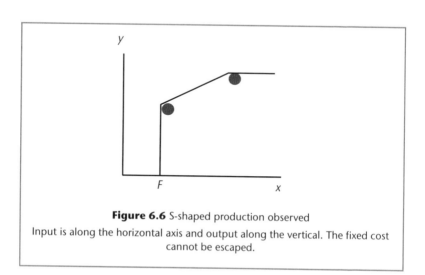

Figure 6.6 S-shaped production observed
Input is along the horizontal axis and output along the vertical. The fixed cost cannot be escaped.

Figure 6.6 features a small decision making unit (the lower dot) and a big one (the upper dot). It is drawn so that the big decision making unit is more productive (more output per input, the line to the origin is steeper), but that does not matter and could have been the other way round. The tenet of DEA with variable returns is that any weighted average of the observed decision making units is feasible. These weighted averages are represented by the line segment connecting the two dots. It is assumed that it is impossible to run single activities at lower intensity. If this were allowed, variable returns to scale would degenerate into decreasing returns to scale, where the line segments connecting the dots with the origin are feasible, as seen in Figure 6.3 (e). The variable returns to scale model also excludes the possibility of running activities at higher intensities. Doing so would take us back to the case of increasing returns to scale, as seen in Figure 6.3 (f).

An implicit but important assumption of DEA with variable

returns to scale is that the hypothetical decision making unit representing inactivity—with zero input and zero output—is ruled out. The reason is simple. If it were allowed, any decision making unit could dissolve its fixed cost by averaging out with the inactivity point (the origin in Figure 6.6), and this trick would take us back to the small-is-beautiful world of decreasing returns to scale, such as in Figure 6.1 (b). The bottom line is that the smallest observed fixed cost is accepted as inescapable.

Let me now discuss the relationship between the analysis of returns to scale and data envelopment. A subtle distinction will emerge. It can be ironed out, but only by introducing even more model variants. The issue is explained easily in the context of the simple Figure 6.6. Perhaps the most natural assumption in this example would be that of decreasing returns to scale, for the small unit has a greater output/input ratio than the big unit. The consequent production function is depicted in Figure 6.7.

Let me explain Figure 6.7. Under the assumption of decreasing returns to scale, any activity can be run at a lower scale as well. This explains the line segment connecting the origin with the small unit and also the one connecting the origin with the big unit. At small levels of input the maximum level of output is

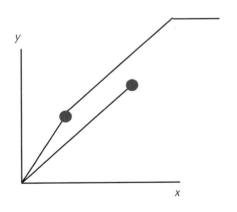

Figure 6.7 Same data as Figure 6.6, but assuming decreasing returns
Input is along the horizontal axis and output along the vertical.

determined by the output/input ratio of the small unit, as it is greater than the output/input ratio of the big unit. Now suppose we command a level of input slightly above the size of the small unit. What is the maximum amount producible? Well, we would first employ the first unit up to capacity, as it is the more productive. The remaining available inputs are employed in the second unit, and increase output beyond the first data point in Figure 6.7, at a rate determined by the productivity of the second data point, which is the slope of the dashed curve. We translate that curve from the origin to the first data point and thus continue the production.

Figure 6.7 shows the needling point between scale economies and data envelopment. For example, imagine the total input is reduced to the input of the big unit: an accident in the small business kills all its workers. Then it would be optimal to relocate workers from the big business to the small business, which is more productive in Figure 6.7. This would increase output. Hence the output of the big business is not the maximum producible output. In other words, the second data point resides *within* the production possibility frontier, and the frontier is *not* the closest envelopment of the data.

This discrepancy between returns to scale assumptions and data envelopment can be resolved, although it is not clear whether that is desirable. Anyway, if we reason as many free market economists do, we would argue that if the big business could produce more it would produce more, and therefore better reside on the production possibility frontier. This mildly dogmatic reasoning can be accommodated by the following modification, which is motivated by the analysis of variable returns to scale. Instead of assuming that each decision making unit's intensity is less than unity (Table 6.1, decreasing returns), we assume that the *total* intensity is less than unity: $\theta_1 + \theta_2 \leq 1$. (This is for two units, as in Figure 6.7. The extension to more units is straightforward.) Under this more restrictive condition, we can speak of *enveloping decreasing returns to scale*, and the production function becomes as in Figure 6.8.

Under enveloping decreasing returns to scale, output expansion beyond the full utilization of the productive small business is

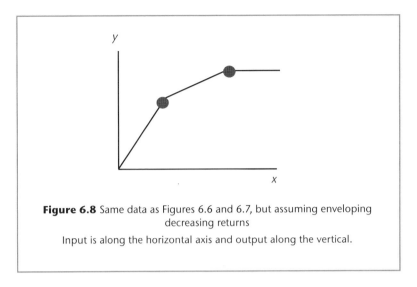

Figure 6.8 Same data as Figures 6.6 and 6.7, but assuming enveloping decreasing returns

Input is along the horizontal axis and output along the vertical.

possible only by simultaneously shrinking the utilization of that same business. This process continues gradually until the next unit is fully utilized and the first, small unit is no longer. Hence the connection between the two data points in Figure 6.8. The consequent frontier is below the one of ordinary decreasing returns, depicted in Figure 6.7. Now the data are enveloped indeed.

The concept of increasing returns to scale can be modified similarly. Instead of assuming that each decision making unit's intensity is greater than unity (Table 6.1, increasing returns) we assume that the total intensity is greater than unity. Under this less restrictive condition, we can speak of *enveloping increasing returns to scale*.

All the forms of returns to scale we have encountered are applicable to organizations with multiple inputs and outputs. The analysis is a bit messy in the framework of production functions (see for example Baumol, 1977), but in the application to benchmarking it becomes pleasantly crisp. The different return to scale cases can be described by alternative restrictions on the intensities with which best practices are run to assess the potential output of a decision making unit. Let us first recall the central tool of benchmarking and then discuss how the alternative returns to scale assumptions can be accommodated. I shall also analyze the implications for accounting prices and their use in ranking.

Benchmarking rests on Chapter 3's program (12). It computes the potential output of a decision making unit, say unit 1, and is reproduced here for convenience:

$$\max_{\theta_1,\dots,\theta_l, e \geq 0} e: \tag{23}$$
$$x^1_1 \theta_1 + \dots + x^I_1 \theta_I \leq x^1_1, \dots, x^1_k \theta_1 + \dots + x^I_k \theta_I \leq x^1_k$$
$$y^1_1 \theta_1 + \dots + y^I_1 \theta_I \geq y^1_1 e, \dots, y^1_l \theta_1 + \dots + y^I_l \theta_I \geq y^1_l e$$

In program (23), the activities of all decision making units $1, \dots, I$ are run with respective intensities $\theta_1, \dots, \theta_I$ such that no more inputs are used than are available to unit 1 (the right-hand sides of the $\leq$ inequalities), and such that the outputs become a maximal multiple of the actual outputs of unit 1 (the right-hand sides of the $\geq$ inequalities). Implicitly, constant returns to scale are assumed.[2]

The first modification we shall consider is *decreasing returns to scale*. Following our discussion and its summary in Table 6.1, we must limit the intensities of activities between 0 and 1. Benchmarking program (23) is modified only slightly and becomes program (24):

$$\max_{\theta_1,\dots,\theta_l, e \geq 0} e: \tag{24}$$
$$x^1_1 \theta_1 + \dots + x^I_1 \theta_I \leq x^1_1, \dots, x^1_k \theta_1 + \dots + x^I_k \theta_I \leq x^1_k$$
$$y^1_1 \theta_1 + \dots + y^I_1 \theta_I \geq y^1_1 e, \dots, y^1_l \theta_1 + \dots + y^I_l \theta_I \geq y^1_l e$$
$$\theta_1, \dots, \theta_I \leq 1$$

Now let us turn to the second modification. *Increasing returns to scale* are accommodated by limiting the intensities of the benchmarks considered to values greater than 1. Now a nasty complication pops up. While in the case of decreasing returns to scale the condition that an intensity of a benchmark must be between 0

---

2   This was discussed in Chapter 3 following the presentation of program (12).

and 1 automatically includes the possibility of ignoring bad examples (by setting their intensities equal to corner value 0), we must now accommodate this possibility explicitly. In other words, we may not simply adopt the constraint $\theta \geq 1$ from Table 6.1, but must include the possibility $\theta = 0$. In this case benchmarking program (23) becomes program (25):[3]

$$\max_{\theta_1,\ldots,\theta_I,e \geq 0} e: \tag{25}$$
$$x^1_1\theta_1 + \ldots + x^I_1\theta_I \leq x^1_1, \ldots, x^1_k\theta_1 + \ldots + x^I_k\theta_I \leq x^1_k$$
$$y^1_1\theta_1 + \ldots + y^I_1\theta_I \geq y^1_1e, \ldots, y^1_l\theta_1 + \ldots + y^I_l\theta_I \geq y^1_le$$
$$\theta_1,\ldots,\theta_I = 0 \text{ or } \geq 1$$

Finally we turn to the important case of *variable returns to scale*. These are modeled by the requirement that the sum of the intensities must be 1. Then benchmarking program (23) becomes program (26):

$$\max_{\theta_1,\ldots,\theta_I,e \geq 0} e: \tag{26}$$
$$x^1_1\theta_1 + \ldots + x^I_1\theta_I \leq x^1_1, \ldots, x^1_k\theta_1 + \ldots + x^I_k\theta_I \leq x^1_k$$
$$y^1_1\theta_1 + \ldots + y^I_1\theta_I \geq y^1_1e, \ldots, y^1_l\theta_1 + \ldots + y^I_l\theta_I \geq y^1_le$$
$$\theta_1 + \ldots + \theta_I = 1$$

Programs (23) to (26) benchmark decision making unit 1 against all units of the organization, and it is obvious how to do the same for the other units. For example, to benchmark unit 2, simply replace the superscripts 1 on the right-hand sides of the inequalities in the programs by superscripts 2.

Since we have a choice between four benchmarking techniques—based on constant, decreasing, increasing, or variable returns to scale—let me discuss the pros and cons of each.

The constant returns to scale model, (23), is the most basic one and the easiest for the determination of accounting prices.[4]

---

3   Recall from Chapter 3, in the discussion following equation (13), that the expansion factor e is at least 1 automatically, so that the nonnegativity constraint on this variable could just as well be dropped.
4   See Chapter 3, formula (15).

Basically it compares the productivity of a unit to the best practice, ascribing any shortage in its output/input ratio to inefficiency. If a best practice unit is small, it may not be realistic to assume it could employ all or many of the resources of the unit we assess. In this case we would do better to adopt the decreasing returns to scale model, (24). It is only slightly more complicated, by the inclusion of the condition that the intensity variables are bound by unity. This condition ascribes some of the inefficiency to the scale effect. The modification of the accounting prices is straightforward and will be demonstrated below.

Conversely, if the base analysis identifies a best practice that is large compared to the unit we assess, it may not be realistic for it to be run at the small scale required to employ the resources of the small unit. In this case the increasing returns to scale model (25) is suggested, but contrary to the decreasing returns model, it is problematic. The difficulty is that the set of intensities over which we maximize—given by $\theta_1, ..., \theta_I = 0$ or ≥ 1—involves discrete choices or jumps (between the values 0 and 1). Solving program (25) involves the selection of all possible benchmark combinations, which is a combinatorial problem with 2^I possibilities, a huge number. Still, once this has been solved it is possible to express the accounting prices in terms of the selected benchmarks, as will be done below.

Although the variable returns to scale model of benchmarking is intermediate—involving increasing returns to scale at low levels of output (due to the possibility of spreading the fixed costs) and eventual decreasing returns to scale—its level of difficulty is not greater, because it does not inherit the combinatorial complication of the increasing returns model. The set of admissible intensities is defined by the simple summing up condition given in program (26), which admits smooth transitions between potential benchmarks. The variable returns to scale model also inherits the property of an S-shaped production function which encompasses the cases of decreasing and increasing returns. Related to this flexibility there is a better fit to the data. In other words, as there is empirical support for S-shaped production functions (or U-shaped average costs), the variable returns to scale model of benchmarking outperforms its counterparts.

The variable returns to scale model can be used to locate decision making units, placing them in the initial region of increasing returns, the intermediate efficient region of constant returns, or the eventual region of decreasing returns.

Case study 9: U.S. real estate investment trusts

Topuz, Darrat, and Shelor (2005, p. 1978) calculated the numbers and the percentages of 235 U.S. real estate investment trusts operating at the different levels of scale economies. They measured inputs and outputs by physical units and by the number and type of transactions or documents processed over a given time period. The inputs were total borrowings, notes, debentures, and repurchase agreements. The outputs were real estate loans made to other parties, properties in operation, and other assets.

The results suggested diseconomies of scale over the period 1989–99, when the percentage of trusts with decreasing returns to scale doubled from 43% in 1989 to 80% in 1999. By contrast, the number of scale efficient (with constant returns to scale) trusts declined from 26% in 1989 to only 2% in 1999. As for trusts with economies of scale, their percentage in the total varied from 62% in 1990 to only 9% in 1993, rising to 60% in 1997, and then falling again to 18% in 1999.

Let me now turn to the implication for accounting prices in each of the models. We have to apply the theory of linear programming (see Chapter 2). I shall take the modifications of the basic model one at a time.

In the *decreasing returns to scale* model, (24), we add the capacity constraints, $\theta_1, ..., \theta_l \leq 1$. We shall denote the shadow prices of these constraints by $\tau_1, ..., \tau_l$. Chapter 3's equation (13) is modified as follows:

$$
\begin{aligned}
(0 \ ... \ 0 \ 1) &\leq w_1(x^1_1 \ ... \ x^l_1 \ 0) + ... + w_k(x^1_k \ ... \ x^l_k \ 0) \\
&+ p_1(-y^1_1 \ ... \ -y^l_1 \ y^1_1) + ... + p_l(-y^1_l \ ... \ -y^l_l \ y^1_l) \\
&+ \tau_1(1 \ 0 \ ... \ 0 \ 0) + \tau_l(0 \ 0 \ ... \ 1 \ 0); \\
w_1&,...,w_k \geq 0 \quad p_1,...,p_l \geq 0 \quad \tau_1,...,\tau_l \geq 0
\end{aligned}
\tag{27}
$$

This modification keeps the price normalization function (14) of Chapter 3 intact, but changes the dual constraint function (15) into:

$$p_1 y^1_1 + ... + p_l y^1_l \leq w_1 x^1_1 + ... + w_k x^1_k + \tau_1, ...,$$
$$p_1 y^l_1 + p_l y^l_l \leq w_1 x^l_1 + ... + w_k x^l_k + \tau_l \tag{28}$$

The main difference from the basic model is that with decreasing returns to scale, accounting prices accommodate *profits*. I shall now undertake some subtle accounting reasoning. The profits are determined by the shadow prices of the activity constraints $\theta_1, ..., \theta_l \leq 1$. By the phenomenon of complementary slackness—Chapter 2's equation (6)—positive profit implies that the constraint, say on decision making units i, must be binding: $\theta_i = 1$. This implies that the nonnegativity constraints for the θ_i's of those units are not binding. This implies—once more invoking complementary slackness—that there is no slack in the shadow prices of the nonnegativity constraints. By the theory of linear programming—see Chapter 2, the transition from equations (10) to (11)—this means that the inequality for such a decision making unit in equation (28) reduces to an equality. In short, profit $\tau_i > 0$ implies equality for unit i in (28). Conversely, inequality for unit i in (28) must yield no profit, $\tau_i = 0$, for otherwise we would have a contradiction! Incorporating these insights, equation (28) may be rewritten as follows:

$$p_1 y^i_1 + ... + p_l y^i_l \leq w_1 x^i_1 + ... + w_k x^i_k + \tau_i$$
$$or \quad p_1 y^i_1 + ... + p_l y^i_l < w_1 x^i_1 + ... + w_k x^i_k \tag{29}$$

The benchmarks for the decision unit we assess fall under the left-hand side of equation (29). On the right-hand side are units which have positive shadow prices of their nonnegativity constraints.[5] By the phenomenon of complementary slackness these units have binding nonnegativity constraints, hence are inactive and, therefore, constitute no benchmark.[6]

In the *increasing returns to scale* model, (25), the benchmarks

---

5   Again, see Chapter 2, the transition from equations (10) to (11).

can be determined in a similar way, albeit we must now consider the many discrete possibilities mentioned before. Let us suppose we have done this, and let $\underline{I}$ be the subset of *active* units i in program (25), for which θ_i is nonzero. The other, *inactive*, units do not contribute to the determination of the maximal producible output, and can therefore be ignored. We shall relabel the units such that the active ones are listed up front, $i = 1, ..., \underline{I}$. The inactive units are $i = \underline{I} + 1, ..., I$. It follows that program (25) may be replaced by its close cousin,

$$\max_{\theta_1,...,\theta_I,e \geq 0} e: \tag{30}$$
$$x^1_1\theta_1 +...+ x^I_1\theta_I \leq x^1_1, ..., x^1_k\theta_1 +...+ x^I_k\theta_I \leq x^1_k$$
$$y^1_1\theta_1 +...+ y^I_1\theta_I \geq y^1_1e, ..., y^1_l\theta_1+...+ y^I_l\theta_I \geq y^1_le$$
$$\theta_1 ,...,\theta_I \geq 1$$

Curiously, program (30) takes us back to the basic benchmarking program, (23), with but one modification: the replacement of the value of the lower bounds, 0, by 1. Now from Chapter 2, equation (5), bounds do not feature in the dual equation. Hence the dual equation is the same as in the basic case, equation (15) of Chapter 3, except for the replacement of I by $\underline{I}$:

$$p_1y^1_1 +...+ p_ly^1_l \leq w_1x^1_1 +...+ w_kx^1_k ,..., p_1y^I_1+ p_ly^I_l \leq w_1x^I_1 +...+ w_kx^I_k \tag{31}$$

Last but not least, let me address the case of *variable returns to scale*, model (26). Mathematically, the analysis follows the decreasing returns to scale case, with two tricks added. The first trick is that we now add a *single* capacity constraint to the basic model: $\theta_1 + ...+ \theta_I = 1$. We denote the shadow price of this constraint by τ. Chapter 3's equation (13) is modified as follows:

---

6   It is possible that $\tau_i = 0$ in equation (29). This corresponds to a benchmark for which neither the nonnegativity constraint (as signaled by the equality) nor the capacity constraint (as signaled by the zero value of its shadow price, τ_i) is binding: in other words the unit is hovering at partial capacity: $0 < \theta_i < 1$.

$$(0 \ ... \ 0 \ 1) \le w_1(x^1_1 \ ... \ x^l_1 \ 0) + ... + w_k(x^1_k \ ... \ x^l_k \ 0)$$
$$+ p_1(-y^1_1 \ ... \ -y^l_1 \ y^1_1) + ... + p_l(-y^1_l \ ... \ -y^l_l \ y^1_l)$$
$$+ \tau(1 \ 1 \ ... \ 1 \ 0); \tag{32}$$
$$w_1,...,w_k \ge 0, \ p_1,...,p_l \ge 0$$

Trick 2 is hidden: there is *no* nonnegativity requirement for shadow price τ in equation (32). This subtle disappearance calls for an explanation.

In the theory of linear programming as developed in Chapter 2, constraints are *in*equalities: see equation (4). The capacity constraint, $\theta_1 + ...+ \theta_l = 1$, fits the theory, provided it is treated as a *pair* of inequalities, $\theta_1 + ...+ \theta_l \le 1$ and $-\theta_1 - ... -\theta_l \le -1$. *Each* of these inequalities has a nonnegative shadow price, which we can call τ_+ and τ_-, respectively. Strictly speaking equation (13) should be modified by augmenting $\tau_+(1 \ 1 \ ... \ 1 \ 0) + \tau_-(-1 \ -1 \ ... \ -1 \ 0)$ with $\tau_+, \tau_- \ge 0$, but that is equivalent to adding $\tau(1 \ 1 \ ... \ 1 \ 0)$ with $\tau = \tau_+ - \tau_-$, an unsigned expression (which can be negative or positive).

Once more, this modification keeps the price normalization function (14) of Chapter 3 intact, but the dual constraint function (15) becomes as follows:

$$p_1y^1_1 +...+ p_ly^1_l \le w_1x^1_1 +...+ w_kx^1_k +\tau, \ ...,$$
$$p_1y^l_1+ p_ly^l_l \le w_1x^l_1 +...+ w_kx^l_k +\tau \tag{33}$$

The main difference from the basic model is that with variable returns to scale, accounting prices admit profits *or* losses. Moreover, compared with the case of decreasing returns, the accounting prices are now such that the profit is uniform across the benchmarks.

The variable returns to scale model is the most popular benchmarking tool. It envelops the data closely, so it reduces the estimates of inefficiency, because the latter is measured by the gap between an observation and the frontier representing potential output. This reduction is considered not bad, because it offsets a shortcoming of DEA, namely its tendency to over-estimate inefficiency. The problem is that DEA is sensitive with respect to errors of measurement, particularly of best practice observations. Overstatement of output or understatement of input may falsely identify decision making units as benchmarks, and as a consequence, throw back the other decision making units. This then suggests that the latter are relatively inefficient, but it is a fluke in the data. This explains the tendency of DEA-based benchmarking to overestimate inefficiency.

Case study 10: European railways returns to scale

In case study 7 in Chapter 4, Coelli and Perelman (1999) found that the European railways were 82 percent efficient, assuming constant returns to scale. Under variable returns to scale the efficiency estimate becomes quite a bit higher, namely 89 percent on average, now ranging from 76 percent in Greece (also the lowest when constant returns are assumed) to 96 percent in the Netherlands and the United Kingdom (which replaced Switzerland). These results confirm the tendency of DEA based on constant returns to scale to overestimate inefficiency: that is, underestimate efficiency.

Further reading

In the economic literature Baumol, Panzar, and Willig (1982) analyze minimum average costs in a multi-output setting, and ten Raa (1983) frees the analysis from non-scale assumptions. The nice work of Førsund and Hjalmarsson (2004) resurrects the minimum average costs analysis in a DEA framework. Once more I recommend Ray (2004) for an accessible introduction. A solid text for the nuts and bolts of returns to scale and other DEA technicalities is Cooper, Seiford, and Tone (2006).

7

CONCLUDING REMARKS

It is an article of faith that profits do not tell the whole story of business performance. Non-financial measures, such as customer satisfaction and personnel commitment, are deemed important for the long-run health of companies, even when that is defined in monetary value terms. Moreover, some organizations are in the "business" of nonprofit activities, so we need to find other performance indicators. In his interesting article "The economics of performance management in nonprofit organizations" Gerhard Speckbacher puts it succinctly:

> The nonprofit has no relatively simple financial goal that can be translated into subgoals and used as a means of communication. Different subunits that produce different goods and services can hardly be compared, because a common language is missing. Whereas profits serve as such a simple common language for communication, delegation, and coordination within for-profit firms, decisions in nonprofits have to be made with reference to the mission.... The objective function of nonprofits generally reflects a variety of different claims, needs, and

interests. Therefore, it is typically nebulous and multidimensional. The technological view is not helpful for transforming a nebulous mission into a performance scorecard.

(Speckbacher 2003, p. 270)

Here the "technological view" considers an organization as a machine that transforms inputs into outputs, where the latter are priced in the market place. Speckbacher is not alone in arguing that the economists' view of the firm as an input–output transformer is useful only if there are markets for all products and services, on both the output and the input side.

This book tells a different story. The theory of benchmarking proves that the input–output model of business *is* powerful even when it is not clear how to value different score components, such as customer satisfaction and staff loyalty. When markets fail to price inputs and outputs, or when markets are missing, they cannot be used to determine the profitability of alternative business strategies. While this is a correct observation, we have seen that the performance measurement tool of benchmarking can be used to construct a substitute, namely shadow or accounting prices. In a sense, such constructed prices are even better, because they closely monitor productivity, whereas market prices tend to be distorted, reflecting subsidies, market power, or other sources of value with no basis in rational management. Moreover, the distortions may be beyond the organization's control, for example when suppliers overcharge. In this case profitability underestimates performance.

Benchmarking is *more* than simple measurement and ranking. It can be used to compare "multi-dimensional" decision making units and to determine the relative importance of these different dimensions, such as sales volumes and quality indices. Accounting prices can be calculated on the basis of non-price information about the outputs and inputs of an organization, and subsequently be used as a basis to assess its efficiency and ranking compared with competitors. Moreover, accounting prices have very useful properties, mimicking pure market prices, including the capacity to decentralize decision making. The value–cost ratio based efficiency measures developed in this book translate company objectives into subgoals. and can be used as a means of communication by the internal benchmarking of divisions.

Key to the results we have established, such as the measurement of efficiency by value–cost ratios and the weighting of the importance of alternative objectives of an organization, has been the simultaneous treatment of the inputs and the outputs of decision making units. Traditional benchmarking, involving comparisons with benchmarks on a piecemeal basis, does not have the capacity to handle essential trade-offs, as between cost reductions and quality improvements. Yet such balancing acts become ever more important in a world where businesses are evaluated on the basis of a variety of scores, financial, environmental, and other. If markets do not price all these scores, we must do it ourselves. Benchmarking is a tool that offers valuations.

I admit that even the method of benchmarking outlined in this book may produce ambiguous outcomes, simply because many choices have to be made. What are the relevant inputs and outputs? How do we model scale effects? Do we use the tool of data envelopment analysis or that of stochastic frontier analysis? We have seen that the Swiss, Dutch, or British railways might be judged best, depending on our modeling assumptions. At the international level of railway companies it is reasonable to presume that errors of measurement and model differences are innocent technical complications in the estimation of efficiency.

We should be alert to the fact that the sensitivity problems become real when business units are benchmarked against other units to determine bonuses for the managers, or when the company as a whole is benchmarked against the competition to determine the bonuses of the corporate officers. There is a clear interest in selecting "favorable" outputs and inputs, misreporting the data so as to overstate performance, or selecting a model that gives the desired results. In well-known cases the temptation has been overwhelming. It is also safe to assume that there are unknown cases where fraud is not discovered, but damage is inflicted nonetheless--in the form of excessive compensation, which is a cost component after all. The upshot is that benchmarking is best treated with caution, and with accounting scrutiny. You are advised to limit its use as a managerial instrument.

When applied carefully, though, benchmarking is a useful tool, including for the determination of the weights to be assigned to competing uses of resources and to the scores of different dimensions. It requires a little work, but there is more to benchmarking than *HPCwire*, the high productivity computing newsletter, suggested:

The only genuinely objective benchmark is the one left on a person's trousers when they sit on a bench that has just been painted.

REFERENCES

Adler, Nicole, Friedman, Lea, and Sinuany-Stern, Zilla (2002) "Review of ranking methods in the data envelopment analysis context," *European Journal of Operational Research* **140**(2), 249–65.

Afriat, S. N. (1972) "Efficiency estimation of production functions," *International Economic Review* **13**(3), 568–98.

Aigner, D. J. and Chu, S. F. (1968) "On estimating the industry production function," *American Economic Review* **58**(4), 826–39.

Aigner, D. J., Lovell, C. A. K., and Schmidt, P. J. (1977) "Formulation and estimation of stochastic frontier production function models," *Journal of Econometrics* **6**(1), 21–37.

Ali, Agha Iqbal and Gstach, Dieter (2000) "The impact of deregulation during 1990–1997 on banking in Austria," *Empirica* **27**(3), 265–81.

Anderson, Randy I., Fish, Mary, Yi Xia, and Michello, Frank (1999) "Measuring efficiency in the hotel industry: a stochastic frontier approach," *International Journal of Hospitality Management*, **18**(1), 45–57.

Banker, R. D., Charnes, A., and Cooper, W. W. (1984) "Some models for estimating technical and scale inefficiencies in data envelopment analysis," *Management Science* **30**(9), 1078–92.

Baumol, William J. (1977) "On the proper cost tests for natural monopoly in a multiproduct industry," *American Economic Review* **67**(5), 809–22.

Baumol, William J., Panzar, John C., and Willig, Robert D. (1982) *Contestable Markets and the Theory of Industry Structure*, Harcourt Brace Jovanovich, New York.

Bogan, Christopher E. and English, Michael J. (1994) *Benchmarking for Best Practices: Winning Through Innovative Adaptation*, McGraw-Hill, New York.

Camp, Robert C. (1989) *Benchmarking: The Search for Industry Best Practices that Lead to Superior Performance*, ASCQ Quality Press, Milwaukee.

Charnes, A., Cooper, W. W., and Rhodes, E. (1978) "Measuring the efficiency of decision making units," *European Journal of Operational Research* **2**(6), 429–44.

Coelli, Timothy and Perelman, Sergio (1999) "A comparison of parametric and non-parametric distance functions: with application to European railways," *European Journal of Operational Research* **117**, 326–39.

Coelli, Timothy J., Prasada Rao, D. S., O'Donnell, Christopher J., and

Battese, George E. (2005) *An Introduction to Efficiency and Productivity Analysis*, Springer, New York.

Cooper, William W., Seiford, Lawrence M., and Tone, Kaoru (2006) *Data Envelopment Analysis: A Comprehensive Text with Models, Applications, References and DEA-Solver Software*, Springer, New York.

Debasish, Sathya Swaroop (2006) "Efficiency performance in Indian banking—use of data envelopment analysis," *Global Business Review* **7**(2), 325–33.

Färe, Rolf, Grosskopf, Shawna, and Knox Lovell, C. A. (1994) *Production Frontiers*, Cambridge University Press, Cambridge.

Färe, Rolf, Grosskopf, Shawna, and Logan, James (1983) "The relative efficiency of Illinois electric utilities," *Resources and Energy* **5**(4), 349–67.

Førsund, Finn R. and Hjalmarsson, Lennart (1974) "On the measurement of productive efficiency," *Swedish Journal of Economics* **76**(2), 141–54.

Førsund, Finn R. and Hjalmarsson, Lennart (2004) "Are all scales optimal in DEA?" *Journal of Productivity Analysis* **21**, 25–48.

Foster, Lucia, Haltiwanger, John, and Syverson, Chad (2005) "Reallocation, firm turnover, and efficiency: Selection on productivity or profitability?" National Bureau of Economic Research Working Paper 11555,

Francis, Graham, Humphreys, Ian, and Fry, Jackie (2005) "The nature and prevalence of the use of performance measurement techniques by airlines," *Journal of Air Transport Management* **11**(4), 207–17.

Gascho Lipe, Marlys and Salterio, Steven E. (2000) "The Balanced Scorecard: Judgmental effects of common and unique performance measures," *Accounting Review* **75**(3), 283–308.

Georgescu-Roegen, N. (1951) "The aggregate linear production function and its applications to von Neumann's economic model," pp. 98–115 in T. Koopmans (ed.), *Activity Analysis of Production and Allocation*, Wiley, New York.

Giménez-García, Víctor M., Martínez-Parra, José Luis, and Buffa, Frank P. (2007) "Improving resource utilization in multi-unit networked organizations: The case of a Spanish restaurant chain," *Tourism Management* **28**(1), 262–70.

Hicks, J. R. (1935) "Annual survey of economic theory: The theory of monopoly," *Econometrica* **3**(1), 1–20.

Kaplan, Robert S. and Norton, David P. (1996) "Using the Balanced Scorecard as a strategic management system," *Harvard Business Review* **74**(1), 75–85.

Kaplan, Robert S. and Norton, David P. (2005) *The Balanced Scorecard: Translating Strategy into Action,* Harvard Business School Press, Cambridge, Mass.

Kumbhakar, Subal C. and Lovell, C. A. Knox (2003) *Stochastic Frontier Analysis*, Cambridge University Press, Cambridge, UK.

Kuosmanen, Timo, Cherchye, Laurens, and Sipiläinen, Timo (2006) "The law of one price in data envelopment analysis: Restricting weight flexibility across firms," *European Journal of Operational Research* **170**(3), 735–57.

Mladjenovic, Paul Stock (2002) *Investing for Dummies*, Wiley Media, New York.

Morey, R .C. and Dittman, D. A. (1995) "Evaluating a hotel GM's performance: A case study in benchmarking," *Cornell Hotel & Restaurant Administration Quarterly* **36**(5), 30–5.

ten Raa, Thijs (1983) "On the cost-minimizing number of firms," *Economics Letters* **12**(3–4), 213–18.

ten Raa, Thijs (2006) *The Economics of Input–Output Analysis*, Cambridge University Press, Cambridge, UK.

Ray, Subhash C. (2004) *Data Envelopment Analysis: Theory and Techniques for Economics and Operations Research*, Cambridge University Press, Cambridge, UK.

Schefczyk, Michael (1993) "Operational performance of airlines: An extension of traditional measurement," *Strategic Management Journal* **14**(4), 301–17.

Simar, Léopold and Wilson, Paul W. (2000) "Statistical inference in nonparametric frontier models: The state of the art," *Journal of Productivity Analysis* **31**(1), 49–78.

Speckbacher, Gerhard (2003) "The economics of performance management in nonprofit organizations," *Nonprofit Management & Leadership* **13**(3), 267–81.

Topuz, John C., Darrat, Ali F., and Shelor, Roger M. (2005) "Technical, allocative and scale efficiencies of REITs: An empirical inquiry," *Journal of Business Finance & Accounting* **32**(9–10), 1961–94.

Watson, Gregory H. (2007) *Strategic Benchmarking Reloaded with Six Sigma: Improving your Company's Performance using Global Best Practice*, Wiley, New York.

Yli-Viikari, Anja, Risku-Norja, Helmi, Nuutinen, Visa, Heinonen, Esa, Hietala-Koivu, Reija, Huusela-Veistola, Erja, Hyvönen, Terho, Kantanen, Juha, Raussi, Satu, Rikkonen, Pasi, Seppälä, Anu, and Vehmasto, Elina (2002) "Agri-environmental and rural development indicators: A proposal," Agrifood Research Reports 5, MAA Agrifood Research Finland.

Yoo, Hanjoo (2003) "A study on the efficiency evaluation of Total Quality Management activities in Korean companies," *Total Quality Management* **14**(1), 119–28.

Zairi, Mohamed (1996) *Benchmarking for Best Practice: Continuous Learning Through Sustainable Innovation*, Butterworth-Heinemann, Oxford.

INDEX